SO YOU WANT TO BE A PRINCIPAL?

William Hayes

ScarecrowEducation
Lanham, Maryland • Toronto • Oxford
2004

Published in the United States of America
by ScarecrowEducation
An imprint of The Rowman & Littlefield Publishing Group, Inc.
4501 Forbes Boulevard, Suite 200, Lanham, Maryland 20706
www.scarecroweducation.com

PO Box 317
Oxford
OX2 9RU, UK

British Library Cataloguing in Publication Information Available

Library of Congress Cataloging-in-Publication Data

Hayes, William, 1938–
    So you want to be a principal? / William Hayes.
        p. cm.
    Includes bibliographical references and index.
    ISBN 1-57886-075-X (pbk. : alk. paper)
    1. School principals–Vocational guidance. 2. Educational
leadership. I. Title.
LB2831.93 .H39 2004
371.2'012–dc22   2003019271

∞™The paper used in this publication meets the minimum requirements of
American National Standard for Information Sciences—Permanence of
Paper for Printed Library Materials, ANSI/NISO Z39.48-1992.
Manufactured in the United States of America.

CONTENTS

ACKNOWLEDGMENTS

I am greatly indebted to Dawn Zegers, a senior teacher-education major, who has been my partner in preparing my last four books. Dawn has been much more than a typist. She has been involved in every aspect of the book and her work has truly made this project possible. Another student office assistant, Katrina Oyer, also helped by working on the index for this volume. As with all of my books, my wife, Nancy, proofread every page and made valuable suggestions to improve the final product. Both Nancy and Dawn have been patient and conscientious contributors to this volume, and I am extremely grateful to them for all that they have done.

INTRODUCTION

Position Opening: School Principal, Anytown School District. Qualifications: Wisdom of a sage, vision of a CEO, intellect of a scholar, leadership of a point guard, compassion of a counselor, moral strength of a nun, courage of a firefighter, craft knowledge of a surgeon, political savvy of a senator, toughness of a soldier, listening skills of a blind man, humility of a saint, collaborative skills of an entrepreneur, certitude of a civil rights activist, charisma of a stage performer, and patience of Job. Salary lower than you might expect. Credential required. For application materials, contact . . .[1]

Although this job description overstates what is expected of a successful building principal, it does capture the qualities and skills that would help someone be effective in the position. Even a partial list of the duties carried out by a building principal is impressive. Some of these actual responsibilities are:

- The ability to articulate the mission of the school in a clear and concise manner.
- To act as the instructional leader of the faculty.
- To help in the selection and supervision of the faculty and staff who work in the building.

- To develop and manage large budgets.
- To maintain a safe and orderly climate for students, faculty, and staff.
- To exercise the responsibility of ensuring a clean and well-maintained building.
- To enforce within the school the policies developed by the board of education and the laws passed by federal and state governments.
- To develop schedules for students, faculty, and staff.
- To supervise extracurricular programs and to be a visible participant at school events.
- To ensure fair implementation of the contracts with employee groups.
- To make recommendations that will be crucial in the decision of whether a teacher will be granted tenure.
- To act as a spokesperson for the school to the entire community.
- To participate in numerous ceremonial functions, including assemblies, pep rallies, honor society inductions, and graduation.
- To act as a mentor and model for faculty, staff, and students.

There are certainly other skills and tasks that could be added, but even this list makes clear the challenges that principals face. However difficult the position might be, research has long shown that successful principals are essential if a school is to be effective. Beginning in the 1970s, studies have again and again agreed on the importance of the principal in their school. Specifically, higher student achievement has occurred in schools where principals do the following:

- Articulate a clear school mission
- Are a visible presence in classrooms and hallways
- Hold high expectations for teachers and students
- Spend a major portion of the day working with teachers to improve instruction
- Are actively involved in diagnosing instructional problems
- Create a positive school climate[2]

Newer research would add some supplemental qualities that are helpful in ensuring the success of a principal. These skills are:

- Recognizes teaching and learning as the main business of a school
- Spends time in classrooms and listening to teachers
- Promotes an atmosphere of trust and sharing
- Builds a good staff and makes professional development a top concern
- Does not tolerate bad teachers[3]

It is not surprising that effective principals make a difference, but many may not realize that the need for principals has never been greater. "Forty percent of the nation's 93,200 principals are nearing retirement, according to the Department of Labor, and 42 percent of the surveyed districts say they already have a shortage of qualified candidates for open principal positions."[4] In many areas of the country, schools are being administered by interim principals. These interim appointments are most often given to retired administrators. For too many schools, their substitute leaders merely attempt to maintain the status quo.

Another concern is the mobility of school administrators. The turnover rate, especially in some areas of the country, is extremely high, and it is not unusual for a school to have three or four different leaders during a decade.

The shortage is also caused by the fact that many teachers do not aspire to the position of building principal. Faculty members watch their leaders struggling with unhappy students, parents, and employees. They hear frequent criticism of their building principal in their faculty rooms and conclude that it is a thankless job. Financially, it is not unusual for someone moving into an assistant principal's position to be asked to take a lower salary than he or she was receiving as a teacher. Another disadvantage that is obvious to most teachers is that school administrators must work during vacations and have numerous evening obligations. Although once it was considered a very natural progression, especially for male teachers, to move on to school administration, that is no longer the case. There is also the obligation to earn extra graduate credits and sometimes even an additional degree in order to be certified as an administrator. All of these factors have led to a reduction in the pool of applicants for the positions of building principals.

Another aspect of the problem is the training program for school administrators. There seems to be a general impression that students entering graduate programs in school administration have not done particularly well, compared to other professions, on the Graduate Record Examinations. There also is general criticism of the college programs currently preparing students for the position of principal.[5] All of these factors do not bode well for the acquisition of outstanding leaders in our schools.

My reasons for writing this book include a desire to provide a fair description of the role of building principals and to discuss the advantages and disadvantages of working in such a position. It is certainly true that not every successful teacher should seek to become a principal. As I explore the challenges and rewards of being a building-level administrator, it is my hope that it will help readers determine whether it is a position and a way of life that would be good for them. Some will undoubtedly decide that it would not be a fulfilling job. On the other hand, if this book leads even a few qualified people into the area of school administration, my efforts will not have been wasted. For me, my twenty-five years as a school administrator represented a calling and provided my family and me with a very satisfying life's work. It is essential for the future of American education that a new generation of leaders steps forward, committed to improving the educational opportunities of our nation's children. To those who have the courage and the stamina to do so, I dedicate this book.

NOTES

1. Michael A. Copland, "The Myth of the Superprincipal," *Phi Delta Kappan* 82, no. 7 (March 2001): 528–32.

2. David Clark, Linda Lotto, and Mary McCarthy, "Factors Associated with Success in Urban Elementary Schools," *Phi Delta Kappan* 61, no. 7 (March 1980): 467–70. It appears in Myra Pollack Sadker and David Miller Sadker, *Teachers, Schools, and Society* (New York: McGraw-Hill, 1994), 246.

3. Bess Keller, "Principal Matters," *Education Week* 18, no. 11 (11 November 1998): 25–27.

4. Craig Savoye, "Fewer Step Forward to Be School Principals," *Christian Science Monitor* 93, no. 216 (2 October 2001): 16.

5. Copland, "The Myth of the Superprincipal."

❶

THE CHANGING ROLE
OF THE PRINCIPAL

We have had principals for most of the history of public schools in America. As we moved from the one-room schoolhouse to larger buildings, it became necessary to appoint a "head teacher" or "principal teacher" to be in charge. Very early, the term *principal* emerged as a way of describing the teacher in charge. This trend was stimulated by the popularity of the Prussian model of graded classrooms, which slowly replaced the practice of having students of all ages working with a teacher in a single room. Horace Mann saw this grade-level model while visiting Prussia in 1843. He wrote in his *Seventh Annual Report* that the problem of having teachers teaching a variety of subjects to different age levels could be remedied. "All these difficulties are at once avoided by a suitable classification, by such a classification as enables the teacher to address his instructions at the same time to all children who are before him, and to accompany them to the playground at recess or intermission without leaving any behind who might be disposed to take advantage of his absence."[1]

The establishment of larger graded schools also led to what one historian called a "pedagogical harem" of a male principal and female teachers.[2] This is a situation that has begun to change in recent years.

Historically, educational administrators have been successful teachers who have been promoted to a leadership role. For the last half century, states have created specific certification for school administrators, which has required additional college training and, in many states, some sort of internship.[3]

In the twentieth century, the importance of the role of the school principal has been recognized in many studies and publications. Typical of an education textbook is the following statement, which appeared in 2002: "The principal occupies the key position in school organization. The school is a social system with belief patterns, authority structures, formal and informal communication systems, special interest groups, etc. and the influence of the principal reaches into each of these elements."[4]

Initially considered primarily a building manager, the principal's position in schools expanded and now includes a number of responsibilities. The U.S. Department of Labor describes these duties as follows:

1. Principals set the academic tone of the school building. They are involved in hiring, evaluating, and helping to improve the skills of teachers and other staff.
2. Principals are part of a district administrative team and also work with students, parents, and representatives of community organizations. Principals must work with all of these groups in making administrative decisions.
3. Principals are responsible for budgets, schedules, and numerous reports.
4. Principals are accountable for students' academic progress and for ensuring that their teachers are following appropriate curriculum.
5. Principals are important in the establishment of a healthy and safe school climate. As part of this responsibility, they must maintain discipline among the student body.[5]

For the better part of the twentieth century, principals have exercised considerable authority over their buildings, teachers, and staff. Beginning in the 1960s, building managers have been buffeted by several major trends in public education. Perhaps one of the most significant has been the development of teacher and staff unions. As various states authorized public employees to organize and to engage in collective bargaining with their employer, many important decisions began to be made during the contract negotiations between unions and the school district. The areas covered in these contracts quickly expanded from salaries and fringe benefits to other "conditions of employment." School districts and unions agreed on language that affected work schedules, free periods, seniority, and other areas that were once controlled by the building principal. Building administrators were often asked for their input, but did not participate at the bargaining table or have a veto power over the contract language that was agreed upon.

As unions became more militant, grievance clauses were written as part of contracts. Principals found themselves as the initial step in complicated grievance procedures. When an employee felt that a contract had been improperly administered, he or she could—with the help of the union—challenge a principal's administrative action. Even when there was not a formal grievance, principals could find a union representative sitting in on their conversations with a teacher or staff member. The union building leader became a competing source of power within the building. Paid professional union representatives might also be brought in to deal with problems within a building. This often was the case during a grievance procedure. As early as 1968, I published an article entitled *Teacher Militancy and the Role of the High School Principal* in which I quoted a National Education Association project entitled "Why Teachers Are Militant." The report talked about the rising educational level of teachers and their desire to be part of the decision-making process within a school. It went on to say "With these changes in the teaching staff, the traditional, paternalistic, all-knowing principal is going to be resented. In fact, it is the failure of this type of principal to allow the competent teacher to utilize his professional training, which is one of the factors that has led to teacher dissatisfaction."[6]

Unions and restrictions made by the courts and legislators caused William Raspberry to write in the *Washington Post* in 1976 that "the combination of judicial restraints and concessions to the teachers' union has eroded almost to the vanishing point the ability of principals to manage their personnel."[7]

Because of conflicting pressures from employee unions on one hand and the superintendent and board of education on the other, principals began to be labeled "middle-managers," attempting to keep everyone happy. Sara Lawrence Lightfoot has argued that the principal is caught between a "bureaucracy expecting efficiency and authoritative leadership and a ferment from below that requires a new style of leadership—open, unguarded, inclusive, and also regarded . . . as more 'feminine' than the traditional patriarchal style."[8] Whether this theory is true or not, it cannot be doubted that the emergence of employee unions has had a dramatic effect on the role of the building principal.

A second trend that has had a great deal of influence on the leadership role of principals during the 1980s and 1990s has been the practice known as "site-based management." Taken from an idea that was first utilized in private industry, the concept is to allow individual school communities—including principals, teachers, parents, and sometimes students—to make more of the decisions that affect their individual school building. The practice will, at least theoretically, alter the typical bureaucratic structure that encourages top-down decision making. States such as New York have gone so far as to mandate that every single public school building have a site-based committee that includes at a minimum teachers, parents, and the school principal. The rationale for the practice is that the people who are most affected by a decision ought to be allowed to participate in what is also called "shared decision making." Secondly, it is argued that once these decisions are made, the so-called stakeholders are more likely to be accepting and willing to carry out the policy.[9]

These school-centered committees can be involved in many types of issues. Discipline policies of a school would be one popular topic, as would discussions on academic eligibility. In some communities, the committee has even participated in hiring administrators and teachers. The results of site-based management are difficult to measure, but there are often problems with the practice. Some of the difficulties are as follows:

1. Finding time for meetings can be an issue. Evenings are often best for parents, but some teachers hesitate to take on an additional evening commitment. Some teacher unions have asked that committee representatives be given release time during the day. Taking a teacher out of a classroom during the school day is not a popular option in many schools. For the principal, whether the

meeting is during the day or in the evening, it is still another obligation. The compromise is often to hold the meetings in the late afternoon when people are tired and look forward to getting home.

2. The interests of the different individuals represented in the committee can be very divisive. As the school district administrator, principals are hesitant to allow any committee to make a decision that might be contrary to their own views. As a result, it is possible for principals to become seen as blocking group action. This is especially true because most committee bylaws or formats do not grant a principal veto power. Faculty representatives on the committees are often chosen by their unions and therefore must represent their fellow members. At the same time, student representatives also feel obligated to voice the opinions of the students who have selected them for the committee. With all of these potential differences, it is understandable that some committees have difficulty reaching a consensus.

3. Perhaps the largest potential problem for the committees is their relationships with the superintendent and the board of education. Despite the fact that the site-based management groups seemingly have significant responsibilities, those projects and policies that require financial support can only proceed with the approval of the superintendent and the board of education. A school committee can work for months on a plan to establish mandatory computer classes for all students, but if the recommendation requires financial support that is not forthcoming, the committee can become frustrated and even lose interest in participation. Unless school-based committee members feel the district is supporting them and that they are participating in meaningful decision making, the process can fail in a district.

In any case, many principals see site-based management as a mixed blessing. They are most likely pleased that decision making is apparently being shifted from the central office to the individual school. On the other hand, this new authority—whether it involves budget decisions, policy, or personnel—must be shared by the principal with the committee. The school administrator's role in such a group is a difficult one. As a single member, who is often not even the chairperson, the principal cannot be seen as trying to dictate to the group. At the same time, he or she needs to help to guide the decision-making process and to provide the necessary information to the group. To be truly effective, the principal has to be able to build a consensus among members who often have differing views. Even though a school district organizational chart indicates that the principal is in charge of the building, the reality is that principals are—for many decisions—facilitators who create an environment for democratic decision making. While principals are not the sole decision makers in a school, they are held as being ultimately responsible for whatever happens in the building.

This responsibility or accountability has grown during the past decade. Principals have always been judged on their effectiveness with student discipline, how well the building is maintained, and the relative happiness of students, faculty, and staff. A principal's success or failure is increasingly hinging on student achievement as measured by high-stakes tests. As states developed specific curriculum standards during the 1990s, it became necessary to ensure that the standards were being met. The resulting tests at all levels have added pressure on building administrators. Many states now require the publication of comparative building test scores. A school that is experiencing declining scores is bound to receive public scrutiny. The importance of testing is highlighted in a publication of the National Association of Elementary School Principals in which the authors wrote, "Virtually every school and student in the nation is gearing up for testing right now. Principals stay close to home and teachers are doing their last-minute drilling. For students these test results may affect their grade promotion or even graduation. For schools and districts, they may cause rewards or punishments."[10]

The No Child Left Behind Act, passed by Congress in 2002, has only increased the emphasis on test scores. This law created mandatory testing for every public school in the United States in grades three through eight. Failure to show improvement on the results of the testing can lead to a loss of federal funds, as well as other penalties under the law.

As a result of the emphasis on academic achievement as measured by test scores, a consensus has emerged that principals must be much more than a building manager. A report released by the National Association of Secondary Principals concludes with these words:

As policymakers in Washington, DC continue talks of reforming public education, raising student achievement, and holding schools accountable, the essential and critical role of a school's instructional leader—its principal—cannot be neglected. The principalship is the core leadership position in America's schools. It is the principal who must exert the leadership skills and instructional acumen to promote school based reform, equity, and excellence for all children. Without instructional leadership and direction, school-based reform will essentially take place one classroom at a time.

For principals to balance their time as building managers with their responsibilities as instructional leaders, they must have relevant preparation and pre-service and in-service professional development; organizational structures and personnel to assist with school management tasks; and resources to support faculty professional development. Leadership will vary from school to school, depending upon the experience, the skills, and the will of the principal as well as the support available in the community. But the focus of every school leader must be teacher instruction and student learning.[11]

As one considers the impact of unions, the emergence of site-based management, and the trend toward academic accountability, it is clear that there have been major changes in the role of the building principal. During the 1950s, principals were seen primarily as disciplinarians and building managers. By the 1960s, as more and more school districts became centralized and districts grew in size, the building principal was eclipsed in larger districts by growing numbers of directors and assistant superintendents. At the same time, the growth of unions also affected the powers and prerogatives of the building principal. By the 1970s, as a result of federal pressure to reform schools, there began to be a focus on the need for change. The Nation at Risk study and other reports charged that our schools were ineffective and that they needed serious reform. Education research that was published at that time strongly supported the idea that an individual school's effectiveness was closely tied to the leadership of the building principal. As we entered the decade of the 1990s, school reform focused on the need to improve the leadership skills of those serving as school principals.[12]

In 2001, the National Association of Elementary School Principals released a report entitled *Leading Learning Communities: Standards for What Principals Should Know and Be Able to Do*. This document introduces six standards that attempt to redefine the meaning of instructional leadership for today's principals. These standards include:

- Leading schools in a way that puts student and adult learning at the center. In addition, principals serve as lead learner and teacher;
- Promoting the academic success of all students by setting high expectations and high standards and organizing the school environment around school achievement;
- Creating and demanding rigorous content and instruction that ensures student progress toward agreed-upon academic standards;
- Creating a climate of continuous learning for adults that is tied to student learning;
- Using multiple sources of data as a diagnostic tool to assess, identify, and apply instructional improvement; and
- Actively engaging the community to create shared responsibility for student and school success.[13]

There is no question that successfully carrying out the responsibility of instructional leadership, along with the traditional role of building manager, is asking a great deal. Still, most principals would agree that the two functions are directly related if the goal is indeed to establish a true "learning community." Although the challenges are great, it is also true that building principals have never been in a better position to truly make a difference for children. Recognizing the magnitude of the job, many districts have created positions for assistant principals and other staff to assist the building leader. With or without extra help, principals are now recognized as a key element in improving our schools.

Although they are currently viewed as important educational leaders, one cannot help but wonder what the future holds for those in the position. Joseph Murphy, chair of the Department of Educational Leadership at Peabody College of Vanderbilt University, has addressed this question and has suggested these "metaphors" for the twenty-first century.

- *The Principal as Organizational Architect:* In addressing the challenges of the changing context in which schools must function, tomorrow's principal will need to learn—and help others to learn—about principles of post-industrial organizations, and assist teachers, students, and parents to reconstruct schools consistent with these principles.

- *The Principal as Social Architect:* The nation's changing social fabric threatens to overwhelm American society in the years ahead, and a feeble response could result in the emergence of a dual-class society like that found in many Third World countries. Schools in the coming century will be a major factor in the adequacy of the nation's response, and principals will have a large role in determining whether the schools' efforts are successful.

  In their role as social architects, principals need to see education as one element of a larger attack on the problems facing at-risk children and give voice to the moral imperative to address these problems beyond the school. To accomplish this, the twenty-first-century principal will need to help design and construct an integrated network of social agencies—possibly with the school at the hub—to address the conditions confronting many students and their families. At the same time, the principal must also redesign the purpose and structure of the school to better serve its changing student population.

- *The Principal as Educator:* Tomorrow's school leaders must provide students with more complex and demanding educational experiences than ever before. At the same time, they must reach a large number of students who have not experienced success even under less demanding standards and expectations. To accomplish this, the principal will need to be more committed to educating children than ever before. Because the challenge for tomorrow's leaders will be to focus the structure of schooling on new educational concepts, the principal will need to be more broadly educated and more knowledgeable about teaching and learning.

- *The Principal as Moral Agent:* As we move into a new century, a major initiative appears to be forming to address the issue of values in education and to recognize the moral dimensions of schooling in general, and of the principalship in particular. At the core of these efforts is a growing acknowledgment of the fact that value judgments are central in selecting and realizing educational goals. Closely aligned with this perspective is a growing acceptance of the fact that the principal's school activities are intertwined with critical ethical issues. At a deeper level, the principalship is being slowly transformed into an instrument of social justice.[14]

This is but one view of the future. No one can be sure of the direction of school reform, but we can safely expect that school principals will continue to be in the midst of the action. This will hopefully entice a significant number of teachers to consider accepting the challenge of leadership.

There can be little question of the need of our society to ensure an ongoing supply of well-prepared individuals to assume the leadership of our schools. That preparation is the all-important subject of our next chapter.

NOTES

1. Horace Mann, "Seventh Annual Report to the Massachusetts State Board of Education, 1843," in *Readings in Public Education in the United States: A Collection of Sources and Readings to Illustrate the History of Educational Practice and Progress in the United States*, edited by Ellwood Cubberley (Boston: Houghton Mifflin, 1934), 287–88, as published in Joel Spring, *The American School 1642–1990*, 2nd ed. (New York: Longman, 1990), 138.

2. Joel Spring, *The American School 1642–1990*, 2nd ed. (New York: Longman, 1990), 138.

3. John D. Pulliam and James J. Van Patten, *History of Education in America*, 7th ed. (Upper Saddle River, N.J.: Prentice-Hall, 1999), 270.

4. Lloyd E. McCleary and Scott D. Thomson, *The Senior High School Principalship*. Vol. 3, *The Summary Report* (Reston, Va.: National Association of Secondary School Principals, 1979), as published in Eugene F. Provenzo, Jr., *Teaching, Learning, and Schooling: A Twenty-first-century Perspective* (Boston: Allyn and Bacon, 2002), 121.

5. U.S. Department of Labor, "Education Administrators," *U.S. Department of Labor Bureau of Labor Statistics Occupational Outlook Handbook*, at http://stats.bls.gov/oco/ocos007.htm (accessed on 1 February 2003).

6. Elizabeth D. Koonz, "Why Teachers Are Militant . . . N.E.A. Report," *New York State Education* 54 (March 1967): 29, as published in William D. Hayes, "Teacher Militancy and the Role of the High School Principal," *The High School Journal* 52, no. 3 (October 1968): 33.

7. William Raspberry, *Washington Post*, 16 July 1976, 27(A), as published in Gene I Maeroff, *Don't Blame the Kids: The Trouble with America's Public Schools* (New York: McGraw-Hill, 1982), 162.

8. Kathleen Cushman, "The Essential School Principal: A Changing Role in a Changing School," *Horace* 9, no.1 (September 1992).

9. Robert F. McNergney and Joanne M. Herbert, *Foundations of Education: The Challenge of Professional Practice*, 2nd ed. (Boston: Allyn and Bacon, 1998), 196–99.

10. Vincent L. Ferrandino and Gerald N. Tirozzi, "It's Testing Time Again," *National Association of Elementary School Principals* 2002, at www.naesp.org/misc/edweek_article_5-08-02.htm (accessed 1 February 2003).

11. National Association of Secondary School Principals, "Priorities and Barriers in High School Leadership: A Survey of Principals," *National Association of Secondary School Principals* 2001, at www.nassp.org/publicaffairs/pr_prncpl _srvy1101.html (accessed 1 February 2003).

12. Anne Turnbaugh Lockwood, "The Changing Role of Principals: An Interview with Philip Hallinger," *North Central Regional Educational Laboratory*, at www.ncrel.org/cscd/pubs/lead31/31hallin.htm (accessed 21 February 2003).

13. National Association of Elementary School Principals, "NAESP Redefines Role of School Principal," *National Association of Elementary School Principals*, at www.naesp.org/comm/prss10-29-01.htm (accessed 21 February 2003).

14. Joseph Murphy, "What's Ahead for Tomorrow's Principals," *National Association of Elementary School Principals*, at www.naesp.org/ comm/p0998a.htm(accessed 1 February 2003).

➋

FORMAL TRAINING PROGRAMS FOR PRINCIPALS

Early efforts to provide graduate education for future administrators were often sporadic and less than effective. My own preparation would offer an example. Prior to taking my first administrative position as a high school assistant principal in 1968, I had taken only two administrative courses at Cornell University. The school district that employed me was a well-paying suburb of New York City and apparently they were satisfied that my experience as a department chairperson for four years in a small district in upstate New York was sufficient. One year later, after taking two additional administrative courses, my twelve hours of graduate study met the requirements for becoming a building principal in New York State, and I accepted a position in a midsize district near Rochester, New York. Still, with only twelve hours of graduate credit in administration, I became the superintendent of the district in 1973 with the promise that I would take an additional twelve hours to gain the proper certification.

All of the classes were chosen randomly, and they were taken at four different colleges. At the time, there were no specific administrative programs or sequenced courses in our area. As long as they were labeled as educational administration classes, they met the requirement. There was also no required internship for certification as an administrator in

New York State. This new element of training was not introduced until
the late 1970s. Even then, most administrative internships were unpaid,
part time, and often limited. I have sponsored over a dozen interns from
several local colleges and found their programs wanting. Some of the interns did their work during the summer months when there were no
students or faculty in the building. At best, these students had the opportunity to work on scheduling, sit in on interviews, and perhaps attend
several board of education meetings. A number of other interns contin-
ued to work as full-time teachers and did their administrative internship
in the hours after their classes were completed. Even as I tried to give
these aspiring principals a variety of experiences, I was aware that there
were school districts where the intern was given a single project that the
school district wished to have completed.

Only one of the interns who worked in our schools was actually paid
by the district for one semester. The young man was able to have a complete assignment and by the end of the semester, was dealing with discipline issues and observing teachers.

Another problem with many of the early intern programs was that the
college supervisors often had so many interns that they seldom visited
the school. As a result, the college supervisors added little or nothing to
the interns' overall experiences.

As I look back on the administration classes that I took in the late
1960s and early 1970s, I especially remember courses dealing with
school finance and school law, which turned out to be quite helpful. On
the other hand, I don't recall that I even had the opportunity to choose
courses that would help me become an instructional leader. Nor do I really remember being exposed to current educational research. Another
concern that I had about my experience was that only one of my instructors had ever been a principal.

The decades of the 1980s and 1990s have seen some improvement
over the earlier requirements, although there is still general agreement
that many, if not most, of the programs that seek to prepare future principals are inadequate. Although states have reworked their certification
requirements for teachers and added mandatory testing, they have been
slow to raise the level of certification requirements for principals. In
1992, the National Association of Secondary School Principals published a report that stated "preparation programs in educational admin-

istration have been locked into modes of thinking and structures of practice that have been overtaken by changes in the environment."[1] The publication goes on to make the following observations about preparation programs for principals:

- Typically, students are inundated with theory but have few opportunities to wrestle with applying educational theory to specific professional problems and challenges. Although some preparation programs strive to etch the relationship between theory and practice in students' minds by offering internships and mentorships, in many cases students are still shortchanged because insufficient time is spent carefully planning, and then supervising, these experiences.
- The potency of internships as a learning tool can also be diluted by a lack of collaboration between professors and field supervisors, insufficient attention to trainees' emotional development and social support, or absence of a specific plan for solidifying trainees' cognitive linkages between theory and practice within the context of the internship (Schmuck 1993).
- Administrator training programs are also found wanting when it comes to preparing students for the hectic pace and varied content of principals' work (Anderson 1991). In addition, strengthening aspiring principals' conflict resolution skills and face-to-face communication skills, and educating trainees about the emotional demands of the principalship are not high priorities in most traditional programs (Anderson).
- Another area frequently slighted is that of helping trainees assess and respond effectively to "human situations" (Schmuck).[2]

Specific suggestions for improving administration programs include such things an additional emphasis on decision-making skills. Role-playing in administration classes can be helpful in this regard. One of the most realistic classroom experiences I had was in a course devoted to contract negotiations. Our small class was divided into two teams. One group represented the school district and the other the teachers' union. The exercise started with a current teacher's contract that each group used to develop proposals for new contract language. We followed the entire process through mediation and fact finding. As a student, I have never been in a class that took its work so seriously. Strong and realistic conflict was present and when it was over, all of the class members agreed that it had been an outstanding learning experience.

Problem-based learning is a method that is gaining popularity in school administration programs. In professions such as law, business, and medicine, students are assigned realistic case studies based on real-life problems that they might face in their work. Some are of an ethical nature, while others require the student to develop strategies to react to a specific set of circumstances. A well-written case study can bring a class alive and cause students to consider all sides of a dilemma that they might later face. Case studies also cause students to utilize knowledge they have gained in other classes, whether they be court cases or financial information. Perhaps the most important result from the use of case studies is to confront future administrators with moral and ethical issues. For instance, how does a principal deal with requests for a reference from a student or employee about whom the principal might have questions? Another example would be a principal's reaction to a teacher candidate who has outstanding credentials but is a known homosexual. Classroom discussions of such issues can engage students and help them to learn how to make difficult decisions.

A variation on the case study method is a program developed by Arnold B. Danzig, a professor in the School of Education at Colorado State University. The approach is called "Leadership Stories" and it provides a tool for "connecting theory to practice."[3]

The process begins when the class chooses a school leader in the community to address the group. Each guest agrees to meet twice during the semester. During the first meeting, students learn about the guest's background and motivation for becoming an administrator. At this time, they talk with their guest about leadership qualities and any other topic the students wish to raise.

The second session is devoted to a "real" school issue that the various guests have faced during their careers.

The problem situation to be studied, according to the assignment, would be discrete rather than on-going and it would involve others inside and outside the school. Problems studied by Danzig's students have run the gamut and have included these: school vandalism, a student fight, a student who threatens suicide, negotiating a teacher contract, a junior high school student who brings a weapon to school, personnel issues, a hostile and violent parent, a drunk student, and a hostage situation.[4]

Experiences in classrooms such as this, along with realistic internships, can greatly enhance a preparation program for prospective administrators. Another approach that appears to have promise is when school districts identify outstanding future leaders from among their teaching staff and help to finance a strong academic training program for them. This can, and often is, done in cooperation with an educational administration graduate school. In such cases, the college or university and the school system can jointly plan the curriculum and the internship. The scheme also has the added advantage of a careful selection process. Unfortunately, one of the current problems with education administration programs is that anyone who has earned teaching certification and is willing to pay the tuition can be admitted to an administration program and is eventually certified. Too many colleges do too little to screen students enrolled in their courses. With a jointly sponsored program, it is also possible that internships can take place in the teacher's own school district. District administrators can be instructors and mentors for these students. The practice of assigning students to seasoned administrators during and after their graduate classes also offers great promise in improving programs for future principals. Districts and colleges who are establishing joint programs should consider allowing the mentor to continue to work with a newly certified administrator during the first year of the initial assignment.

It is not only school boards that are seeking ways to ensure qualified leaders for their schools. The public has become increasingly aware of the need for providing preparation programs for school principals. The July 7 edition of the *Los Angeles Times* carried the following headline: "Better Pay, Training for School Principals Urged." The article talked about a privately backed school reform group called LEARN that published a plan seeking to have the Los Angeles school district spend $33 million, which would be divided between salary enhancements and training for the 900 city school administrators. The purpose of the program would be to offer opportunities for leadership training for practicing and potential principals.[5]

In January 2003, the National Staff Development Council also called for new training opportunities for principals. The 10,000-member organization published a report entitled *Learning to Lead, Leading to Learn: Improving School Quality through Principal Professional Development,* which states that "Up to now, principals have been the missing link of the reform movement. . . . We have talked a lot about what teachers can do and what students should be doing, but we seem to have forgotten that it's the principal who sets the tone for a school. Principals today face a daunting task, and we aren't providing the kind of support that will ensure their success."[6]

Currently, there are a number of serious efforts by individual school districts to train future principals. The Cincinnati Public Schools will spend $835,000 to prepare a new generation of school leaders. It is the goal of this program that there always be an available cadre of qualified individuals ready to assume the position of a building principal in the city's seventy-six schools. Cincinnati is taking seriously the U.S. Department of Labor prediction that 40 percent of the nation's 93,200 principals are nearing retirement.[7]

Because of the obvious need for qualified candidates and the dissatisfaction with many of the current programs for preparing principals, a number of innovative approaches are emerging. New York City is looking to John F. Welch Jr., a former CEO of General Electric to help guide the city's initiative for developing outstanding principals. The mayor and the chancellor of the school district expect Welch to be a tough taskmaster. He brings a record to the job that includes eliminating those managers who score in the bottom 10 percent of the performance evaluations. New York City Education Chancellor Joel Klein has taken Welch's advice and announced that he will try to remove the fifty poorest-performing principals.[8] Bringing in a well-known leader to work on educational reform is only one of the approaches being attempted.

The National Association of Elementary School Principals has opened its membership to aspiring building principals. After paying a $65 annual fee, an individual preparing to become a principal can receive the same benefits as the organization's members. They can attend national conventions, receive publications of the organization, and attend two special workshops designed for aspiring principals.[9]

To guide those responsible for preparing training opportunities for future building administrators, several professional organizations, including the National Association of Secondary School Principals, have created performance standards for principals. The first significant publication was developed by the National Policy Board for Educational

Administration. In the report, twenty-one key proficiencies for principals were identified. Following on the heels of this important publication, the Interstate School Leaders Licensure Consortium (ISLLC) developed standards that have been incorporated into a full-day test, which is required in five states for those seeking certification as an administrator. Eighteen other states in the consortium have endorsed these standards.[10]

Not surprisingly, technology is also being used to prepare school administrators. The Department of Education Leadership at Winona State University has been offering graduate administration programs using technology for over ten years. Because of the great distances some students might have to drive to take administration classes, technology has become an attractive alternative in states such as Minnesota and Wisconsin. Especially with content-based courses, such as school law or finance, this approach seems to be a good way to convey essential information. Although students have rated these programs quite positively, students also frequently add comments such as this: "I felt that there was an overload of information with very little time to discuss all of it. More class time to process with peers would have been great. . . . Not enough time to meet as a class."[11] Even though there may be certain courses that can be delivered using educational television or the Internet, most faculty members agree that the face-to-face discussion in the classroom is an essential component of an administrator's education.

The Northwest Regional Lab is pioneering another promising approach. This research-based program offers five content standards for a yearlong program to train future principals. The standards include the following.

1. Vision building—The purpose of this portion of the curriculum is to help individual students develop their personal beliefs and values. If our principals are to lead others, it is important that they have their own vision of what a school should be.
2. School climate—This section of the training helps future administrators develop a school environment in which learning will flourish.
3. Curriculum—The goal of this section of the training is to help students articulate learning goals and to align curriculum and assessment to these goals.

4. Improving instruction—A principal must understand the variety of instructional techniques available to teachers and be able to instruct teachers in their use.

5. Monitoring school performance—Schools must know if they are reaching their educational goals, and the principal must accept the responsibility for not only establishing goals and programs but monitoring them with an effective assessment program. Once assessments are completed, the principal must help the faculty make the necessary adjustments to improve instruction.[12]

While studying various training options, state governments have also been attempting to amend certification requirements for principals.

The state of Massachusetts has worked with Harvard University to develop a graduate program that would lead to state certification. Already Massachusetts has signed reciprocal agreements with a number of states, which allows graduates of the Harvard program to become certified in states other than Massachusetts.[13] Most other states have accredited college administration programs that meet the academic requirements for administrative certification. In some states, there is the added requirement of passing an examination. Students who are planning to study school administration should be certain that the courses they take are acceptable for certification purposes. The best solution, if it is available, is to be part of a graduate program that has already been accredited by the state. For instance, Washington State University has developed a state-approved preparation program. Still, it is true that the state of Washington, like many other states, is currently reexamining its certification requirements for principals. The qualifications that are now required in the state of Washington are typical of many other states. To be a principal in Washington, one has to take the following courses:

EDAD 516	Instructional Leadership	3 Semester Hours
EDAD 583	Community and Communications	3 Semester Hours
EDAD 585	Financial Management in Education	3 Semester Hours
EDAD 588	Law and Education	3 Semester Hours
EDAD 589	Leadership Development Seminar	3 Semester Hours
EDPSY 510	Assessment of Learning	3 Semester Hours
EDAD 590	Internship	6 Semester Hours

Plus 1 Credit on Diversity	1 Semester Hours
Total Semester Credit Hours	25 Semester Hours

°Note: A minimum of a master's degree in a relevant area of study is required for all administrator certificates.[14]

A question being debated in the states of Washington and New York, as well as in other places, is whether a principal should have to earn a master's degree in educational administration. For many teachers aspiring to become a principal, this would require a second master's degree. In New York State, beginning in 2004, all new teachers will need to have a master's degree within three years of receiving their bachelor's degree. Since most potential principals do not begin taking administration courses until after a few years of teaching, the requirement for a second master's degree in administration might discourage some potential candidates. New York State has not announced whether a master's in administration will meet the mandate faced by all classroom teachers under their new teacher certification requirements.

Initial certification requirements in Missouri are also quite similar to those required in other states. For example, for secondary principals, the following requirements must be met:

A. A permanent, or professional, Missouri secondary teaching certificate.

B. A minimum of two years teaching experience in grades 7–12 approved by the Department of Elementary and Secondary Education.

C. Successful completion of the Building Level Administrator's Assessment Test.

D. Completion of a course in psychology and/or education of the exceptional child (two semester hours).

E. Completion of a master's degree in educational administration, or in a certifiable area recognized in Missouri, from a college of university meeting approval of the Missouri Department of Elementary and Secondary Education.

F. Recommendation for certification from the designated official of a college or university approved by the Missouri Department of Elementary and Secondary Education. This recommendation shall be based upon the completion of a planned program for preparation of secondary principals, which includes at least twenty-four semester hours of approved graduate credit in education courses focused upon administration and supervision of the secondary school. The approved graduate credit shall include:

1. Specific courses (must be separate graduate courses of at least three semester hours)
   - Foundations of educational administration
   - Secondary administration
   - Secondary curriculum
   - School supervision
2. Directed field experiences in secondary administration of at least three semester hours.[15]

Some school boards have found certification requirements, such as those in Missouri, too restrictive and have petitioned the state to offer districts more flexibility in hiring principals. There are those who believe that we would do better hiring school leaders who had already proven themselves in other fields. The practice of hiring school administrators from business and government is increasing in larger districts, with mixed results. A much-beloved former superintendent of the Seattle City Schools, the late John Sanford, was a retired major-general and county executive before being hired as superintendent in Seattle. The successful career of this charismatic leader was featured in a PBS feature entitled "A Tale of Three Cities." The program also told of the trials of a former minister and lawyer, David Hornbeck, whose tenure as a superintendent in Philadelphia was characterized by strife and gridlock. At this point, it is too soon to evaluate the effectiveness of hiring educational leaders whose experiences have been outside of the educational establishment.[16]

The National Association of Secondary Principals is concerned enough about the alternative recruitment and certification of principals that they have issued a list of "guiding principles" for such programs. Some of these guidelines include the following:

- Selection of principals must be based on qualities of instructional leadership rooted in established knowledge and skills that result in dedication to good instructional practice and learning.

- Principals, as professionals, are charged with the coordination, facilitation, and implementation of instructional programs, curricula, pedagogical practice, and assessment models—all in the service of teaching and learning.
- A principal must demonstrate the instructional leadership skills and exercise the instructional acumen necessary to promote school-based reform, equity, and excellence for all children.
- Principals, as instructional leaders, understand and implement best practice and participate in intellectual discourse on teaching and learning.
- Only principals who fully understand the teaching–learning process will enhance student achievement.
- School reform will not occur if school districts decide to recruit, appoint, and reward individuals only for their basic management and administrative skills.[17]

As can be seen by these very restrictive guidelines, the principals' group is suggesting very little latitude for hiring those whose careers have been outside of education. At the very least, such individuals currently would have to undergo significant preparation programs. Such curriculums are emerging for meeting teacher shortages. Career changers with strong subject matter background are being prepared for teaching assignments in abbreviated programs. Whether the same type of options will occur for administrators is not clear, but it is evident that practicing administrators have serious questions about recruiting principals from outside the ranks of teachers. The argument for doing so with superintendents is perhaps stronger. As chief school officers, they are ultimately responsible for the finances of the district. Superintendents with strong business backgrounds can hire instructional leaders, while it is expected that principals will be the academic leaders of their buildings. It would probably be safe to predict that alternative certification programs for principals will not in the near future replace the traditional programs. We can expect that most of our principals will continue to come from the ranks of our teaching staffs.

A unique problem in the preparation of principals is to properly train those who will be working in urban areas. Because these schools are indeed different, a special curriculum called "New Leaders for New

Schools" has been established in Chicago. It offers a yearlong, full-time internship for candidates selected from a large pool of applicants. The fifteen individuals chosen were not all teachers and ranged in age from twenty-seven to fifty-two. The students spent time in classrooms in both Chicago and New York City prior to their yearlong internship in city schools.[18]

Whether it is training principals for urban, rural, or suburban schools, colleges and state education departments are grappling for the best way to prepare our future principals. As we enter the twenty-first century, it is very likely that despite the shortage of qualified candidates, these programs will become increasingly demanding. Because the dimensions of the job have grown, it is essential that we prepare men and women who can be both effective managers and instructional leaders. Even though more demanding programs will undoubtedly make it more difficult to be certified, we must seek to do a better job of preparing our future building leaders. Although formal training is important, it alone will not gain a person a position as a principal. Those individuals who wish to be considered as serious candidates for a principalship must build a résumé that clearly demonstrates their ability to lead.

NOTES

1. Linda S. Lumsden, "Prospects in Principal Preparation," *ERIC Clearinghouse on Educational Management*, 1992, at www.ed.gov/databases/ERIC_Digests/ed350726.html (accessed 17 December 2002).

2. Lumsden, "Prospects in Principal Preparation."

3. Gary Hopkins, "Follow the Leader: School Principals in Training," *Education World*, 1998, at www.education-world.com/a_admin/admin048.shtml (accessed 1 February 2003).

4. Hopkins, "Follow the Leader: School Principals in Training."

5. Doug Smith, "Better Pay, Training for School Principals Urged," *L.A. Learning Exchange*, 1999, at www.lalc.k12.ca.us/essay/7_16_99/learnlatimes.html (accessed 1 February 2003).

6. National Staff Development Council, "New NSCD Report Outlines National Strategy for Principals to Bolster Skills, Urges School Leaders to Spend More Time Observing Teachings and Classrooms," *National Staff Development Council*, at www.nsdc.org/leadership.html (accessed 1 February 2003).

7. Andrea Tortora, "CPS Board Considers Program to Train Prospective Principals," *The Cincinnati Enquirer,* 24 February 2003, at http://enquirer.com/editions/2001/01/18/loc_cps_board_considers.html (accessed 24 February 2003).

8. Abby Goodnough, "Executive Who Saved G.E. Is to Train School Principals," *The New York Times,* 14 January 2003, at www.nytimes.com/2003/01/14/nyregion/14PRIN.html?pagewanted=print&position=... (accessed 14 January 2003).

9. National Association of Elementary School Principals, "NAESP Opens the Doors with a Unique Membership Opportunity: The Aspiring Principals Program," *National Association of Elementary School Principals*, at www.naesp.org/npa/aspire.htm

10. Larry Lashway, "Trends and Issues: Training of School Administrators," *Educational Resources Information Center,* 1999, at http://eric.uoregon.edu/trends_issues/training/index.html (accessed 1 February 2003).

11. Lee Gray, "A Hybrid Approach to Web-Delivered Courses: Preparing Principals and Superintendents," 1999, at http://naweb.unb.ca/proceedings/1999/graylee/graylee.html (accessed 1 February 2003).

12. Robert E. Blum, Jocelyn A. Butler, Nancey L. Olson, "Leadership for Excellence: Research-Based Training for Principals," *Educational Leadership*, (September 1987): 25–26.

13. The Principals' Center at Harvard University, "Concentration in School Leadership: Principal Certification Patter," *The Principals' Center at Harvard University*, 2002, at www.gse.harard.edu/principals/about/certification.htm (accessed 13 January 2003).

14. "Administrator Certification Programs—Principal, Superintendent, and Program Administrator," at www.educ.wsu.edu/NCATE/documents/Administrator%20Certification%20Programs.htm (accessed 1 February 2003).

15. Missouri Department of Elementary and Secondary Education, "Certification Requirements for Secondary Principal," *Missouri Department of Elementary and Secondary Education*, 2000, at www.dse.state.mo.us/divteachqual/teachercert/adm712.html (accessed 1 February 2003).

16. William Hayes, *So You Want to Be a Superintendent?* (Lanham, Md.: Scarecrow Press, 2001), 24.

17. National Association of Secondary School Principals, "Alternative Recruitment and Certification of Principals," *National Association of Secondary School Principals*, 2001, at www.nassp.org/publicaffairs/ps_alt_rcrut_crt_prn.htm (accessed 1 February 2003).

18. Alan Richard, "Urban Principal's Program Debuts," *Education Week* 21, no.1 (September 2001): 1–2

❸

PREPARING FOR LEADERSHIP

When seriously considering the possibility of becoming a school principal, it is important to seek leadership opportunities. There are two significant reasons for attempting to have these types of positions. First, and most obvious, is the need to gain experience in leading others. It is essential that anyone aspiring to be a principal have as much practice as possible in forming and guiding groups of people. The second major reason for having these experiences is to begin building a résumé. Anyone seeking to hire a supervisor or building manager will look for what the person has done prior to seeking a position as a principal.

Especially in the current climate that emphasizes the academic accountability of building principals, it is also essential that future leaders demonstrate their interest in curriculum and mentoring teachers. A résumé should include numerous examples of staff development training in curriculum and techniques of instruction. As a teacher, a future principal should be actively participating in workshops and in-service courses dealing with topics that reflect an ongoing interest in classroom instruction. Whether it is multiple intelligence, reflective teaching, or training in the use of instructional technology, future leaders should be attempting to learn as much as possible. Even more impressive on a résumé is the inclusion of conference presentations or publications on academic issues. A candidate who is a respected and knowledgeable leader in areas of instruction demonstrates his professional capabilities by being chosen as a speaker or by being published in educational journals. Such a candidate will have a great advantage over one who has not developed credentials as an informed educator. This type of background will not only enhance a résumé but also help prepare a candidate for the inevitable questions about student learning that will be raised during the interview process. As the academic leader of the school, one must be conversant in all areas of the curriculum and in current educational research. Without this background, a person is not well prepared for the modern role of a school principal.

Just as it is important for every teacher to have experience with children prior to assuming a faculty position, principals should also have multiple examples of ways they have worked with students. Experiences as a camp counselor, a volunteer or paid tutor, or as a Sunday school teacher provide evidence that one is interested in young people. For many who review résumés, volunteer activities with children are especially impressive. As a college student, future educators should, if possible, make choices on summer jobs that will give them the opportunity to work with children.

Perhaps the most important listings on the résumés of future principals involve leadership roles. Becoming the chairperson of a district or building faculty committee or assuming a leadership role with the Parent-Teacher Association demonstrates a willingness to take on responsibility. Even membership on building level or, better yet, district-wide groups can enhance a faculty member's reputation in the district. Site-based management committees offer a chance for future administrators to work with parents.

Visible leadership roles within the community create a favorable impression for someone seeking to enter educational administration. Working as a leader of community improvement projects by a civic organization will give one exposure outside the educational arena. Leadership responsibilities in agencies such as the United Fund or Boy or Girl Scout troops can be helpful. One can also show leadership potential within a neighborhood church. The value of such experiences for advancing one's career will depend on the prestige accorded the group within the community. It may well be that activity with some fraternal orders might not be as helpful as membership in service organizations, such as the Rotary or Kiwanis club. In any case, visibility working as a leader of positive causes and projects can only raise the community status of a future administrator.

One area of leadership that must be approached carefully by future school administrators is one's activity within the school's teacher union. If, as a union leader, a person is viewed by the administration and board of education as an overzealous union militant, it is unlikely that such a person would be sought after as an administrator. On the other hand, if one's union activities reflect that you are not only respected by your colleagues but that you have also demonstrated some empathy for the district's concerns, union activity might be helpful. A future candidate for an administration position should avoid gaining a reputation as an unreasonable advocate of teacher rights. It might be wise to steer away from participation in unpleasant contract negotiations and concentrate instead on projects that have the union and the district working together. Such committees might include groups in which union representatives work with administrators to plan in-service or mentor programs.

An additional experience that can be helpful is to serve as a mentor to teachers new to the district. Many school systems have developed plans that pair experienced teachers with nontenured faculty. Acting as a mentor for one or more new instructors can be a rewarding and invaluable experience for a future instructional leader. At times, mentors also have the opportunity to do informal classroom observations. Although these observations do not usually involve formal evaluation reports for tenure purposes, they do give mentors the opportunity to assist new teachers. Since principals are expected to spend a significant amount of their time supervising and evaluating teachers, the experience of being a mentor teacher is bound to be helpful.

Even with varied leadership experience in one's own district, only about 25 percent of current principals are able to move directly from the classroom to the principal's office. It is more likely that our future building leaders will first serve in other leadership roles.[1] At the elementary level, one might move from a grade-level leader, while in the secondary school the stepping stone might be department chairman or assistant principal. Approximately 50 percent of the building principals in New York State first served as an assistant principal.[2]

Because so many individuals are promoted from assistant principal to principal, it is important to become familiar with the typical job descriptions of assistant principals. Too often, districts use assistant principals solely as disciplinarians. When an administrator's duties are this narrow, the experience can be of limited value as preparation to take a building principal's job. For assistants who are effective as disciplinarians and who enjoy it, the position can represent a lifelong, enjoyable career working directly with students. Many school disciplinarians make a positive difference in the lives of their students. For those who see the job as a "stepping stone," it is hoped that the position will offer a wide range of duties. These responsibilities should include teacher observations, experiences working with the community, and opportunities as a leader of academic committees. With approximately half of our future principals serving first as assistants, it would seem prudent that districts make a conscious effort to broaden the leadership opportunities within their schools and communities.

Whether one is moving from assistant principal or directly from the classroom, it is increasingly true that successful applicants have participated in a program for aspiring principals. As early as 1993–1994, 39 percent of the public school principals had taken part in an aspiring principals program. Of those who had held their jobs for less than four years, 50 percent had been prepared in such a program. The percentage of minority principals who have been part of special training programs is even higher.[3] As noted in the previous chapter, such experiences come in different forms. A program for aspiring principals can be sponsored solely by a school district or in cooperation with an area college or university. Various professional organizations have created their own opportunities for aspiring administrators; some of these have been funded by state and federal grants.

Probably the fastest growing types of programs for future administrators are those where the district chooses and prepares selected teachers. One of the complications for such programs is that those who participate must also meet state certification requirements. The double requirement of taking college courses for certification as well as participating in district programs can be asking a great deal of those aspiring to be principals. This is the reason for the popularity of state-sponsored plans, like the one in Ohio that incorporates college participation in curriculums that are especially designed for school districts, but also satisfy certification requirements.[4]

It is important for potential principals to determine the best time in their teaching career to begin to seek administrative certification. Résumé building can start as a high school student and continue through college. When teachers assume their first teaching position, the aspiring administrators among them should never forget that they are preparing themselves for leadership. Today, many states require teachers to obtain a master's degree or at least additional graduate courses to be fully certified as a teacher. It remains an unanswered question whether states requiring an advanced degree for teaching certification will in the future allow that requirement to be met by earning a master's degree in educational administration. Many future school administrators, very early on in their career, earn a master's degree in their teaching field. This is done before their decision is made to seek administrative certification. Thus, elementary teachers might do their initial graduate work in reading or special education and a secondary degree in their content area. Doing so will undoubtedly broaden their academic preparation as future instructional leaders.

In any case, it is probably not wise for most twenty-two year olds (first-year teachers) to immediately begin taking administration courses. A forty-year-old career changer who has some management experience might wish to move more quickly into educational administration. Whatever a person's future plans, a first-year teacher should give priority to establishing himself or herself as an effective instructor. This is more difficult to do if one is taking a heavy load of graduate courses of any kind.

A more appropriate time to begin administrative course work might be after receiving tenure, during one's fourth or fifth year of teaching. At that point in one's career, a position of a department head or grade-level chairperson might be within reach. Although there are those who achieve their first appointment as a principal prior to age thirty, this remains an exception rather than the rule. In a New York study, the typical principal had thirteen years of teaching experience.[5]

There are also those who choose to go beyond the master's degree to earn a doctorate. Certainly, a candidate with a doctorate has an advantage, but proven leadership capability will undoubtedly be more important to most districts. The doctorate is most useful for those aspiring to a superintendency in a large district. This fact is not mentioned to dissuade individuals who wish to become principals from seeking to earn an advanced graduate degree, but only to point out that a doctorate is not required for principals, even in our most prestigious schools.

One other aspect of preparation is the need to have a number of respected individuals who are prepared to act as personal references. Beginning with college professors, student teaching supervisors, and past employers, one needs to consciously develop relationships that are close enough that a number of people will feel comfortable recommending an aspiring administrator for a position of leadership. For practicing teachers, the principals and superintendents they have worked with are perhaps the most important references. Community leaders, including members of the board of education, are also helpful. Clergymen can be respected references. Although references from one's college can be convincing, any list should include individuals whose status will be noted by those considering the application. Without a group of outstanding recommendations, one's opportunity for advancement in the profession will be limited. Finalists for a principalship will have their backgrounds checked carefully by any school district that is considering them. If someone is applying from outside the district, he or she should expect current supervisors to be contacted.

How does one develop a list of reliable references? As a college student, it is helpful to make a point to get to know your favorite professors. This is especially true of those who teach classes in areas in which one excels. If you spend time with an academic advisor, it is possible that this individual might get to know you well enough to be an effective reference. Supervisors or employers on or off campus can also be used. To prove that one is an effective teacher, the reports from master teachers and college supervisors should be positive.

A teacher working in the school district should attempt to connect with a practicing administrator in the system who can act as a formal or informal mentor. This person can become an advocate within the district as well as a valuable reference. Graduate school professors, especially in the field of education, can also help students during their search for an administrative position.

Teachers who move from one district to another should make a conscious effort when leaving a school to do so in a way that will cause people in their former district to speak well of them. Leaving bad feelings in a district can come back to haunt someone who is seeking a leadership role.

Armed with solid educational preparation, a résumé that includes numerous helpful experiences, and a selection of favorable references, administrative candidates are now ready to consider seeking their first position. The challenge of obtaining that first administrative job is the subject of our next chapter.

NOTES

1. Erikah Haavie, "Good Principals Scarce," *Poughkeepsie Journal*, 24 February 2003, 1(A).

2. Haavie, "Good Principals Scarce."

3. Karen DeAngelis and Robert Rossi, "Programs for Aspiring Principals: Who Participates?" *National Center for Education Statistics* (February 1997): 1–2.

4. Suzette Lovely, "Developing Leaders from Within," *Thrust for Educational Leadership* 29, no. 1 (September/October 1999).

5. Haavie, "Good Principals Scarce."

4

GAINING AN APPOINTMENT

Assuming that one has the appropriate academic preparation, certification, and a strong résumé, the search for that first position can begin. As a person considers breaking into the field of educational administration, it is helpful to be aware of the job prospects. In considering this issue, it is beneficial to know something about those who are currently serving as school principals. There are a number of sources of such information, but perhaps one of the best is a ten-year study completed by the National Association of Elementary School Principals in 1998. Almost fourteen hundred principals responded to this nationwide survey. Some interesting characteristics of the elementary principals in the study were as follows:

- The average age for beginning a career as a principal was thirty-six.
- The average age for those currently serving as principals was fifty.
- The average years of experience in education was twenty-five.
- The average workday was ten hours.[1]

A more recent survey was done in New York State, which found the following:

- The typical principal had thirteen years of teaching experience prior to being appointed as an administrator.

- Nearly half of all principals started as a principal in the district in which they were employed at the time, while 38 percent took positions in schools within commuting distance. Only 12 percent relocated to accept their first position.
- Of the 671 New York principals responding to the survey, 48 percent expected to retire by 2006.
- In this survey, the average age of the principals was fifty-one.[2]

Someone entering a new position would most likely also appreciate knowing something about the salary they might expect. The Educational Research Service came up with the following figures for the 2001–2002 school year:

Position	Average Annual Salary
Elementary school principals	$73,114
Middle school principals	$78,176
Elementary school assistant principals	$60,672
Middle school assistant principals	$64,375[3]

There is also a difference in average salaries, depending on the geographic location of the school. With an average salary of $73,114, the differences are considerable.

Region	Amount
New England	$76,579
Mideast	$87,338
Southeast	$67,458
Great Lakes	$74,476
Plains	$66,455
Southwest	$64,352
Rocky Mountains	$63,048
Far West	$85,385[4]

Most principals had at least a bachelor's degree and, depending on size and level, over 5 percent had doctorates. Almost all principals—98.8 percent—had been teachers, while 54.1 percent had either served as an assistant principal or program director. Female principals have become increasingly more prevalent among those recently appointed. In 1988, 80 percent of the principals were male; ten years later, it was 58 percent. During the past five years, 65 percent of those appointed as principals have been female. In 1994, 83 percent of all principals were white, 10.8 percent were black, and 4.5 percent were Hispanic.[5]

From these figures, one can surmise that, given the average age of our current school principals, there will be numerous opportunities for building administrators. It would also seem that women are becoming principals at an increasing rate. A major survey conducted in 1998 by the Educational Research Service summarized its findings as follows:

> The results of this exploratory study on the possibility of a shortage of qualified candidates for the principalship support the contention that there is cause for concern. Half of the district administrators interviewed felt that there had been a shortage of qualified candidates when they filled at least one principalship in the last year. Factors they feel are most likely to discourage qualified applicants from applying include a level of compensation that is inadequate compared to the responsibilities of the job, job-related stress, and too much time required. These factors were similar for all three levels of schools—elementary, junior high/middle, and senior high—and for all urban, suburban, and rural communities.
>
> Recruiting minority candidates was reported more often as an issue than recruiting female candidates, with fewer of the districts reporting that they had qualified minority applicants than qualified female applicants. Although more urban districts reported that they had qualified minority applicants for the position of principal, it was also more likely to be an issue for these districts than those in other types of communities.
>
> Only about one-fourth of the districts reported the existence of an aspiring principals program to recruit and prepare candidates, a type of "grow your own" approach in which there has been increasing interest expressed recently. Just under half of the districts have a formal induction or mentoring program for new principals.[6]

Another article, entitled "The Shortage of Principals Continues," begins with these words:

> Too many schools opened this fall without a principal. In Vermont, one of every five principals has retired or resigned since the end of last school year. In Washington State, 15 percent of principals did the same last year.

And in New York City, 163 schools opened with a temporary school leader. Cities and states nationwide report principal vacancies and only a trickle of applicants, if any, to fill the positions.

   If we don't stem the flow of retirees and buoy up the numbers of aspiring principals, we will face a crucial school leadership crisis—one that we believe will take a toll on student achievement.[7]

In addition to the overriding problem of the demand for new principals, this article, along with many others, points specifically to the need for additional principals representing minority groups. Currently, only 11 percent of the principals are African American. Even though women have been moving into the position rapidly, the number of minorities acting as principals has not been increasing.[8] With an ever-increasing number of minority students in our public schools, it would seem that it might be helpful, especially in our urban areas, to find ways to recruit more minority principals.

   Whatever one's race or gender, an aspiring principal should be aware of what districts are looking for when they seek a building administrator. An article published by the College of Education at the University of Oregon emphasizes that superintendents and boards of education are looking for a "good fit"—that is, a candidate's apparent ability to mesh with the personalities, culture, and needs of a particular site.[9] Some states also feel that examinations for future administrators will help screen the applicants.

   Kenneth and Miriam Clark (1996) cite evidence that using a carefully chosen battery of tests along with other information provides better prediction of success than using professional judgment alone. Unfortunately, while there are a large number of paper-and-pencil instruments that measure generic management and leadership skills, relatively few have been designed with school leadership in mind.[10]

It is not likely that pretesting for principal job applicants will become a major trend. The process in most districts begins with a review of the paperwork and credentials. This is normally followed by the checking of references and a series of interviews. If one were to generalize about the usual procedure for filling a vacancy in a district, the process often would be as follows:

1. The superintendent and board establish a screening committee of teachers and possibly parents. This could be done either with a joint committee or separate committees. At the high school level, it is possible that student representatives are included in the group.

2. The committee develops or reviews the current job description and perhaps develops a profile of the ideal candidate. This work might be done after a survey is conducted among teachers and/or parents. In smaller districts, the board of education or superintendent might carry out these duties.

3. Once the superintendent and the board approve these documents, the district advertises the position, both within the district for internal candidates and in various professional publications and colleges and universities that have administrative preparation programs.

4. If there is a committee, they review the applications once they begin to arrive. Where no committee is established, central-level school administrators review the applications. It is usually the administrator's job to check references of candidates being seriously considered.

5. Although districts might receive numerous applications, only perhaps five to ten will be invited for an initial interview. These interviews can be conducted by the committee or by district administrators.

6. Following the initial screening, the field is narrowed down to two or three finalists who might be asked to come to the district for a full day of interviews.

7. If the candidate is from outside the school district, it is possible that either the committee or a school administrator would visit the candidate's current school during the process. Such visits would include conversations with administrators, teachers, and possibly students and community members in the candidate's district.

8. During the final full-day visit, finalists are likely to have sessions with faculty, parents, possibly students, the superintendent, and in smaller districts, the board of education.

9. Following this final visit, and possibly additional reference checks, those involved in the process will make a final choice. In the end, the superintendent and the board of education make the decision.

10. The superintendent then notifies the successful candidate and sets up a meeting to discuss the conditions of employment. These would include such issues as salary, fringe benefits, professional growth opportunities, and the evaluation procedure. If the district's principals have a formal organization or union, most of these issues will be dealt with in the unit's contract with the district. With principalships that are not covered by a contract, individual negotiations are necessary. A successful candidate should use this meeting to gain a complete understanding of the conditions of employment; if there is not a contract, the candidate should ask that these conditions be put in writing.

11. Following an agreement between the candidate and the district, the school often has a formal reception to welcome the new principal. At that time, if the new principal is married, it is not unusual for the spouse to be invited to the reception.

Let us now return to the beginning of the process to consider how candidates should conduct themselves during this sequence of activities. When submitting a letter of interest in a position, candidates should be careful in writing the initial letter. It should not appear to be a form letter that is being sent out to every district with a vacancy. The cover letter should introduce the candidate and include several reasons why the applicant is interested in this particular job. In addition, any letter of application should attempt to highlight several factors that might capture the attention of whoever is screening the applications. The accompanying résumé and perhaps the college placement folder should emphasize the academic and work experiences of the applicant. If there is a written application for the position, it should be neat and carefully prepared and any essay section should be edited to ensure that it is totally free of error. The letter to the district should be sent to the superintendent, making sure that the name is correctly spelled.

When one is invited for an initial screening interview, it is essential to learn as much as possible about the district. Even inside candidates need to prepare carefully. Some of the issues to be considered are as follows:

1. In finding out about a school district, an applicant can begin with the district website. For those coming from outside, taking time to

read back issues of local newspapers can be helpful. Talking to residents of the district, especially friends, can provide useful information. It is especially interesting to learn about the history of the principalship in the school. Is the vacancy caused by the retirement of a longtime incumbent? What is the reason for the present principal's decision to leave? If possible, one might find out something about the reputation of the person leaving the job. Following a longtime, popular principal can be a difficult challenge for any aspiring administrator; if faced with this situation, one must develop a strategy. On the other hand, following an administrator who has been unsuccessful is often easier, as people are more than ready for a change.

2. The candidate should also review the questions likely to be raised by the interviewing committee. In order to give articulate answers in these areas, the applicant must have developed views on such topics as inclusion, student discipline, making schools safe and secure, methods for improving academic results, ways to support and evaluate personnel, and the role of teachers, staff, and parents in managing schools. Candidates should be prepared to talk about their philosophy of education. Any current topics, such as high-stakes testing, the No Child Left Behind Act, or any specific issues that are plaguing that particular district should be questions an applicant should be prepared to answer. If applicants can find out before the interview what such issues might be, it will give them an edge in responding to questions that are important to that district. One should be ready to discuss in the most modest way possible any previous accomplishments and personal strengths. At the same time, it would not be unusual to be asked to identify weaknesses. Needless to say, this can be a difficult question, and it is important not to highlight weaknesses that might have a negative effect on one's candidacy. Finally, at some point in the process, an applicant is likely to be asked if he or she intends to live in the school district. Although fewer and fewer districts mandate district residency for their principals, especially in rural areas, board members and some superintendents see it as a positive factor. Prior to going to any interview, candidates should discuss this issue with their families.

3. The applicants should also be prepared with a list of questions to
   ask at any interview. Below are some suggestions.
   - Is there a written job description for building principals? If
     there is not, candidates should ask those conducting the inter-
     view what they see as the primary responsibilities of building
     principals in that district.
   - One might ask about the organizational chart in the district.
     Which employees report directly to the principal? For instance,
     do the building custodians report directly to the principal or
     to the superintendent of buildings and grounds? Who is the
     immediate supervisor of building principals? Is it an assistant
     superintendent or is the principal responsible directly to the
     superintendent?
   - What site-based management teams have been established in
     the district? What is the make-up of these teams? Does the
     principal chair the building team? Is the principal a voting
     member of the team? How successful have these teams been to
     date?
   - Does the school have an active parent organization?
   - In addition to the faculty, what other instructional personnel are
     working in the building? Are there remedial reading instruc-
     tors? Does the school have teacher aides? Who directly super-
     vises the aides?
   - Are the board and the community satisfied with the school and
     the students' academic progress?
   - Does the school have assigned grade-level leaders or depart-
     ment chairs? If so, what are their duties?
   - What is the principal's role in the district budget process?
   - Are the building principals in a negotiating unit that has a con-
     tract with the district, or does each individual principal negoti-
     ate terms and conditions of employment with the district?

Some of these questions are appropriate for an interviewing committee, although others should be saved for discussions with the administrative personnel of the district. The general rule would be that anything
involving terms and conditions, evaluation, or the organizational chart
probably should be saved for discussions with administrators.

Questions related to contract terms and conditions will usually be discussed in detail with the superintendent after an offer is made. That is the appropriate time to discuss salary, fringe benefits, and opportunities for professional growth. It is also important to know how one's work will be judged and if there is a tenure process. Many states do offer tenure protection to principals, but this is not true in all states. Successful candidates should also inquire about the length of any probationary period and the means used to evaluate their work. Is it done solely by the superintendent or the assistant superintendent? Do faculty, staff, parents, or even students participate in the process? In certain districts, a more elaborate system is in place. Some boards of education have attempted to develop merit systems for principals. If such a plan is being discussed, it is hopeful that administrators will participate in its development.

As anyone reviews the process for selecting new principals, it is undoubtedly true that the paperwork that is submitted and one's references are important in getting to the final stages of the hiring process. Still, it is equally apparent that the candidate's conduct during interviews is crucial. Persons seeking to be appointed to their first principalships must prepare for interviews in the same way they might for a final examination in a difficult course. If the applicant is chosen, it means that representatives of the district feel that this person is the right one for this principalship at this particular time in the school's history. It is important that anyone offered a position also share this feeling before agreeing to a contract. One should be extremely cautious about accepting a position when there is doubt that it is a good fit.

Finally, most people during their careers will not be offered every job for which they apply. Although being turned down for a position is almost always disappointing, candidates must not feel that it is a personal failure. The appropriate conclusion is that this particular job was not a perfect fit for them. Many future administrators are candidates in a number of districts before being appointed to their first position as a principal. Gaining that first appointment is just the first step in succeeding. The first twelve months of one's employment as a building principal will be crucial. This is the topic we consider in the next chapter.

NOTES

1. National Association of Elementary School Principals, "Profiling the Principalship: New 2001–2003 Salary Statistics," *National Association of Elementary School Principals*, 2003, at www.naesp.org/prinpro.htm (accessed 1 February 2003).

2. Erikah Haavie, "Good Principals Scarce," *Poughkeepsie Journal* 24 February 2003, 1(A).

3. National Association of Elementary School Principals, "Profiling."

4. National Association of Elementary School Principals, "Profiling."

5. National Association of Elementary School Principals, "Profiling."

6. National Association of Elementary School Principals, "Is There a Shortage of Qualified Candidates for Openings in the Principalship? An Exploratory Study," *National Association of Elementary School Principals*, 2003, at www.naesp.org/misc/shortage.htm (accessed 1 February 2003).

7. Gerald N. Tirozzi and Vincent Ferrandino, "The Shortage of Principals Continues," *National Association of Secondary School Principals*, 2000, at www.nassp.org/publicaffairs/views/prin_short1000.htm (accessed 1 February 2003).

8. Leslie T. Fenwick and Mildred Collins Pierce, "The Principal Shortage: Crisis or Opportunity?" *National Association of Elementary School Principals*, 2001, at www.naesp.org/comm/p0301a.htm (accessed 17 December 2002).

9. Educational Resources Information Center, "Trends and Issues: Training of School Administrators," *Educational Resources Information Center*, at http://eric.uoregon.edu/trends_issues/training/02.html (accessed 1 February 2003).

10. Educational Resources Information Center, "Trends and Issues."

5

THE FIRST YEAR

In any new job, the first days, weeks, and months are crucial. This is especially true for someone in a leadership position. Because individual students, faculty, staff, and parents do not often interact with a principal, their initial contact with a new building administrator colors their perceptions. Whether one is moving into the principalship in his or her own building or coming from outside the school, it is important to make positive first impressions.

It is inevitable that a new principal will be speaking to groups, in assemblies, in faculty and staff meetings, as well as at sessions of the PTA. One should not attempt to "shoot from the hip" with these groups. The student body should come away from their first meeting with the principal thinking that the new administrator seems like "a nice person who wants to do well in our school, but who will not stand for any monkey business." With students, the best possible impression is that their new principal really likes and cares about students and is committed to seeing that the school is safe and orderly.

The faculty, on the other hand, needs to see their leader as one who will support them when there is a problem and also as a person who will be the intellectual leader of the school. Teachers today expect their principal to be not only a good manager but also a master teacher. A new principal will not succeed unless the faculty learns to respect him or her for administrative skills as well as a sincere commitment to improve teaching and learning in the school.

Secretaries, custodians, and other staff should know that the principal respects and appreciates their roles. Not only must expectations for each job be made clear but the building manager should also be open to suggestions and advice from staff members. Many school administrators will ask secretaries their opinions on job candidates who come to the office. The impression one makes on a secretary tells something about a candidate's personality. Staff members should be made to feel that their opinions are valued. A successful principal will always say thank you to staff members for their services and will frequently write notes of gratitude to those who have done something special. Copies of these communications should always be sent to the staff member's direct supervisor, and it should be noted that the letter will be placed in the personnel file. This type of positive feedback early in one's tenure shows that a new principal appreciates good work.

With the first contact with parents, building principals must demonstrate that they are approachable. During one's early days in the school, it is essential that everyone who comes in contact with the new administrator feel that this person is a good listener. People can tell when someone is really listening.

Although there will be paperwork and materials to be read, new administrators should spend the vast majority of their time early on in their tenure talking with people. This should be done even if it is necessary to take work home. A new principal must be visible in the building and in the community. Dropping in on classes, sharing a coffee break with the custodians, and having lunch with the faculty, students, and staff is extremely helpful. One of the worst things that can be said about a principal is that he or she is never seen out of the office.

New administrators should attend as many evening and late afternoon events as possible. Concerts, plays, and athletic events are important community occasions; as the building leader, the principal must be visible. Organizations in the district should be made aware that as a new principal, you are available to speak at their meetings. Many new building administrators hold parent open houses, have informal receptions, or make individual appointments. As building leaders, they should be accessible and not be seen as individuals who manage by memo or e-mail. Personal contact with people is essential, especially during one's first days on the job.

Although new principals may feel compelled to share their personal visions for the school with the faculty and the community, it is prudent not to initiate major changes until one has the opportunity to talk with many people within the school. At the point where the new administrator feels that he or she has a good understanding of the problems in the school, district, and community, and also has an idea of how others perceive the problems, it is time enough to think about change. If the proposals are likely to be at all controversial, a prior conversation should take place with the principal's supervisor. In any case, it is best to establish a level of trust with colleagues prior to attempting to engineer major changes in the school.

There are special problems for those administrators who are promoted to the principalship in their own school. Having already developed a personal relationship with fellow faculty members, staff, students, and parents, as the new principal, those relationships will change. Even though administrators are looked at differently, prior friendships and other relationships cannot change too quickly. A person taking on a new responsibility should not all of a sudden appear to others as someone who "isn't the same." The fact that the person has been promoted from within the organization assumes that the new principal has already earned the respect and possibly the affection of those who work in the school. To suddenly be perceived as a person who now appears to be "uppity" or to have "forgotten his or her friends" can be a disaster for a new administrator.

On the other hand, as a new building manager, principals will be responsible for supervising and evaluating friends and colleagues. The ideal situation would be that these individuals would still refer to their new boss by the person's first name in private, but will use the proper title (Mr., Mrs., Ms., Dr.) in the presence of students and parents. In any case, the responsibility of being in charge of a building will inevitably alter relationships. Principals must maintain absolute confidentiality in dealing with those who are being supervised. It goes without saying that teachers will talk about their principal in faculty rooms and in other venues. It is not unusual when a building administrator enters a faculty group, especially when it is a group of union leaders, that conversations might come to a halt or the subject will quickly change.

Socially, if the principal is known to spend a great deal of time outside of school with certain teachers or staff, there might well be talk among others about the "principal's favorites." As a result, some longstanding friendships might be strained as many principals choose to limit their out-of-school socialization with those whom they supervise to large group activities, such as school picnics or retirement parties. Because friendships are an important part of anyone's life, new administrators may well find that they are becoming closer to other administrators inside and outside of the district. At the same time, it is also helpful to have friends who have nothing at all to do with education. Active participation in church and community activities helps this to occur.

Even if one has worked in a school for many years, there will still be much to learn during the first year on the job. An excellent source of information is the school secretary. These individuals will be used to working with another supervisor whom they might respect and miss. A new principal needs to be sensitive to the advice and concerns of all of the office personnel. If these individuals develop a respect and a commitment to the newcomer, they can help to ensure a principal's success. Because principals tend to work closely with their secretaries, open communication is essential.

A new administrator moving into an unfamiliar school also has unique challenges. There is much more to learn, more people to meet, and a need to make a positive impression on a large number of people. Demonstrating a cheerful and positive approach to others, listening carefully, and praising those who are helpful and doing good work are good techniques. It is especially important to be careful about what one says—both in public and in private. As the leader of the school, a new principal's words can quickly become a topic of the school gossip. New managers must learn to be very careful about what they say, especially before they fully understand their new organization. Changes must take place only after new principals are aware of current conditions, and then it is necessary to build a consensus of support with those affected by the change. A first-year principal who moves too quickly can develop a group of detractors in a very short time.

School districts can assist new principals in avoiding tactical errors during that first year. Some districts have formed a formal or informal mentoring program for new administrators. An experienced practitioner is appointed to help advise and comfort a new building-level leader during the probationary period. Even when no formal mentor program exists, new principals should seek out an experienced administrator (either inside or outside the district) in order to avoid errors early in their career.

The first year of a building principal's administration will be exciting, but it also can be stressful. Taking the time to learn as much as possible about the school and the district can only help. At the same time, administrators must accept the fact that they will make errors of judgment, but these can be minimized if they are not too proud to seek the help of others. It is especially important to develop an honest and trusting relationship with one's immediate supervisor. Superintendents do not like to hear about problems in a school from a parent or read about them in the newspaper. When there is a potentially controversial issue that might become a public controversy, it is best to talk with the central office before the problem becomes a source of conversation in the district. For first-year principals, it is far better to consult with one's supervisor than to try to make decisions in isolation. Just as some first-year teachers sometimes wrongly see asking for help as a sign of weakness, some administrators also hesitate to seek advice. This can be a bad mistake. A building principal can only have a healthy relationship with the central administration and the board of education if a concerted effort is made to make it happen. This is the issue that is addressed in chapter 6.

6

WORKING WITH THE
CENTRAL ADMINISTRATION
AND THE BOARD OF EDUCATION

Principals are middle managers. As such, they have a large number of constituencies whom they must attempt to satisfy. Like any other administrator in a district, they have been formally hired by the board of education based on the recommendation of the superintendent. The superintendent, or perhaps one of the assistant superintendents, will primarily be responsible for supervising and evaluating building principals. Other employees, students, and the public naturally think of principals as "in charge" because they are members of the district management team. In fact, for people connected primarily with one school, the principal is by far the most visible member of the district administration.

This closeness to faculty, staff, students, and parents sometimes creates for principals pressures not experienced by administration in the central office. It is also true that unless building principals are sensitive to the concerns of these groups, they can quickly lose support in their building. A principal who loses the confidence of the faculty can expect the superintendent and board to rapidly become concerned. The same could happen when parents or students become extremely critical of a principal.

There are certain behaviors that are likely to cause principals trouble. Constantly assigning blame to others for difficult situations can backfire on any administrator. A tendency among some building principals is to blame the board of education when talking to faculty, staff, or students. At the same time, when discussing a matter with the superintendent or the board, some principals tend to point fingers at the teachers, the unions, or unruly students. This is especially true during periods of conflict within the district. Grievances by union members can create such situations.

First of all, the best way to deal with grievances is to avoid them whenever possible. When a difficult decision must be made concerning a clause in an employee contract, it is best for a principal to check with the superintendent prior to making a decision. With particularly complex issues, it might well be determined to consult the school attorney. If then the administration does make a decision that is contrary to the union's interpretation of the contract, the district should be prepared to defend itself. Too many unnecessary grievances occur because principals make decisions without knowing that they are violating the contract. It is essential that administrators be fully informed on the exact wording in every labor contract.

Because building principals hear grievances either at the first or second stage of a typical grievance procedure, prior consultation with one's supervisor can help avoid having one's decision overturned later in the process by the superintendent or the board of education. Although grievances can be divisive, there are some situations that the district must see through, even though it might mean an expensive arbitration hearing. Districts certainly should try to find solutions as early in the process as possible in order to avoid prolonged and stressful meetings, as well as expensive attorney fees.

Another time when the principal is likely to be caught in the middle between the board of education and the faculty and staff is during the preparation of the annual budget. Especially when cuts must be made, it is easy for the administration to blame the board for failing to provide the money necessary to fully finance the school's program. The fact is, principals are frequently at least part of the discussion that leads to the decision to make cuts; even if they are not, it is unwise to portray the board as being unwilling to support quality education. Such remarks, even in private, can prove detrimental to a building principal. Instead, administrators should attempt to explain the financial dilemmas faced by the district. If there must be a villain, it is better to point to the un-willingness of the legislature and the governor to provide adequate state aid. At the same time, when talking to board members, it is not the best strategy to assign blame to the faculty and staff for unreasonable demands or for wasting money. A far better role for a principal is to help these potential rivals to better understand the other's position. During the budget process, the one strong position a principal must take is to ensure that the faculty and staff at the building level have sufficient input into the budget. An administrator should not dictate exactly how art teachers and music teachers should spend their allotment. With the budget, as with other issues, faculty should feel a degree of autonomy with their own program.

There is a third area that can cause middle managers to find themselves in a precarious position. In those schools where contracts are negotiated between the school district and employee groups, the principal often is not actively involved in determining the contract language. Most districts rightly avoid having a principal act as a negotiator with the district's unions. This is a time-consuming task and one that building principals should avoid whenever possible. Along with the demands on a building administrator's time, negotiations can cause those sitting at the table representing the district to be targeted as the enemy. At the same time, principals should be very involved in developing the district's position on the proposals and should be consulted on contract language that affects their ability to manage their buildings. If the district is considering allowing every teacher to have an hour of free time each day instead of forty-five minutes, building principals must be included in the discussions. District negotiators can make serious errors if they are not working closely with those who are directly managing the buildings. Principals must take a strong position in ensuring that they are part of these discussions.

During difficult negotiations, the building principal will be caught between the two parties. Teachers may complain about the stubbornness of the district, while board members talk about the unreasonable or selfish unions. During such conflicts, building administrators will have private opinions that are sympathetic with one group or the other. At such times, it is inappropriate to criticize the board and unwise to fuel the anger of board members by being critical of the union.

In some areas where labor disputes include picketing, working to rule, or even strikes, principals have the responsibility of enforcing the contract and the law in their buildings. At such times, they must act as part of the management team. If this means calling the police for clearing the entrances of those who are picketing, the principal must act.

The principal's role is complicated in districts where the administrators themselves are unionized. This is a trend that began in larger districts and has now spread to other districts, even some with fewer than five principals. At times, the administrative unions will also include assistant principals and other district managers, except for superintendents and assistant superintendents. As a middle manager who is also a union member, principals can also become alienated from the board, especially during negotiations. Even though administrators create unions, it does not erase the fact that they are managers and responsible to the superintendent of schools and ultimately to the board of education. Despite one's sympathies with other unions, the principal must enforce district policy and employee contracts. Failure to do so can have dire consequences for a principal.

Along with conflict situations, there also is the responsibility given to some principals to attend meetings of the board of education. In smaller districts, building administrators might be sitting at the table with board members and participate actively in the discussions. In midsize districts, principals might be brought in as consultants on certain issues or be asked to give a report at a meeting. Principals in larger cities might never be asked to speak at a board meeting. Whether one is a regular participant or an occasional guest at meetings, it is essential that principals remember that the superintendent is the chief school administrator. The superintendents should meet often enough with their building administrators so that everyone is aware of the administration's policy. Whether or not principals are informed prior to meetings of the strategy for each agenda item, board meetings are not a time to surprise or embarrass one's boss. If a principal has differences of opinion with other administrators, especially the superintendent, this issue should be discussed in private, rather than publicly.

Individual board members or even other administrators can cause problems for principals. People do attempt to use their position to influence a principal's decision making. It can be a request for a student worker job during the summer with the maintenance department, a plea for intervention with a teacher, or special consideration in a disciplinary manner involving an official's child. When board members ask for special favors, it places any manager in a difficult situation. To succumb to pressure, especially in hiring, can rightfully lead to charges of "favoritism," while indignantly refusing a request can create a powerful enemy. Principals placed in compromising positions should consult with the superintendent prior to making a decision. It is likely that, whatever the issue, the superintendent could later become involved. The best decision is to find the least painful way to not grant special favors to influential people.

Given all these potentially difficult situations, it is a challenge for principals to sort out where their loyalties lie. There is no question that principals can be advocates for faculty and staff within the councils of the administrators and the board. In deciding one's position on important issues, an essential question to ask is "What is best for the students?" This will not always help, because sometimes choices have to be made between groups of students. Is it better to cut a classroom position in the seventh grade and to raise class size from twenty-one to twenty-six, or to abolish the middle school wrestling and volleyball programs? Principals make decisions that have a lasting impact on others on a daily basis. In doing so, they must always remember that they are members of the district management team. Because of this reality, they must not view the superintendent and the board as the enemy, but rather as partners in creating positive educational opportunities for children. As the board and superintendent should not be thought of as adversaries, neither should the faculty and staff. It is with these individuals that principals must work, if they are truly to make a difference in the lives of students.

7

THE PRINCIPAL'S RELATIONSHIP WITH THE FACULTY AND STAFF

Like the relationship with the superintendent and the board of education, a principal's rapport with the building faculty and staff is crucial to succeeding in the position. An administrator who stays in one place for a significant number of years has the opportunity to know many of the teachers in the school from the time they are first recruited to the district. Selecting the best possible teacher for a vacancy is perhaps one of the most important functions of any principal. To find the very best begins with an active recruiting campaign. School districts are wise to advertise their positions in places other than the local newspaper and area colleges. This is especially true if the district is seeking diversity in their faculty. To do so, it might be necessary to send representatives to job fairs and colleges where significant numbers of minority teachers are likely to be present. In any case, using Internet sources along with college and university placement services can offer a wide geographic area from which to recruit a large and varied pool of candidates.

When a district is selecting new faculty, care should be taken to define the skills and qualities that are necessary for the position. Even then there will be barriers to finding and retaining the best possible teachers. A number of these were identified in a two-year study conducted by the

National Commission on Teaching and America's Future. They included the following problems:

- Unenforced standards for teachers;
- Major flaws in teacher preparation;
- Painfully slipshod teacher recruitment;
- Inadequate induction for beginning teachers;
- Lack of professional development and rewards for knowledge and skill; and
- Schools that are structured for failure rather than success.[1]

Despite these potential pitfalls, successful districts are able to find ways to recruit and hire excellent teachers. Gary Hopkins, the editor-in-chief of *Education World*, spoke with a number of principals who identified the characteristics they were looking for when they interviewed potential teaching candidates. Those traits that turned up again and again were passion, enthusiasm, sensitivity, heart, and humor.[2]

The level of participation of building principals in choosing teachers is not the same in every district. If principals find themselves working in a district where there is little or no input, they should seek to become more involved in the process. There is no question that they will be held accountable for successful teaching, and it is only fair that they play a major part in choosing faculty. In some districts, particularly smaller ones, the principal and perhaps a committee will narrow down the candidates to two or three and the superintendent will make the final choice. If a building manager is involved with this system, he or she should ensure that only qualified candidates are sent to the superintendent. In other districts, district-wide personnel departments narrow down a pool of candidates and principals are asked to select their teachers from this group. When this is done, more than one principal in the district might want to hire a candidate, and the teacher is given a choice as to which appointment to accept. Finally, there are schools where the principal is the key person—in a few cases, the only one—involved in selecting a single candidate to be recommended to the superintendent. The most common practice is for a team of teachers to help the principal in selecting final candidates. At the elementary school, it might be a grade-level team; at the middle or high school, department members in

the teacher's academic discipline would make up the committee. Whatever the method used, several suggestions can help in the recruitment
and selection process.

Beginning with the interview, administrators often make the mistake
of talking too much. Although it is important to give the candidate the
opportunity to ask questions, the crucial aspect of an interview is to allow applicants to talk about themselves. Anyone conducting interviews
should develop a series of open-ended questions, based on the qualities
desired for the position, as well as the job description. Every candidate
should be asked the same questions. Especially if the position is at the
secondary level, a specialist in a subject area field should be part of the
interview team. This individual's primary task would be to attempt to
judge the candidate's knowledge of the subject area. When the school
has a department chairman, this is normally a function of that position.

Along with a well-structured interview, school districts should thor-
oughly check the references of all final candidates. Telephone calls to
references allow an administrator to ask more probing questions and
also to add follow-up questions. Many references will feel more comfortable speaking frankly in a phone conversation. Even if the district
sends out prepared reference forms, a telephone contact could be used
to supplement the written form. Pressing references for any weaknesses
the applicant might have or any reservations they might have about hiring the person can elicit some valuable information. Whenever possible,
it is always a good idea to check with people who are not listed as references on the application or who are not part of the college placement
file. If a person is coming from another school district, the principal
might call friends who work in the district. More can be learned about
recent college graduates by calling friends and acquaintances who might
have taught the student. Too many school districts do only perfunctory
reference checks and later discover problems that could have been un-
covered.

Once a candidate is chosen, the principal must ensure that the individual is given a thorough orientation to the district. In some districts,
this consists solely of a one-day meeting for new teachers prior to the
opening of school. During this session, the new instructors are unfortunately bombarded with handbooks, handouts, and advice—and go home
overwhelmed. The failure of districts to appropriately orient and guide

new teachers has undoubtedly been a factor in the high turnover rate of new teachers. A principal would be wise to establish a yearlong series of group and individual meetings with new faculty members to ensure that communications continue throughout the year. Along with the principal's work with new faculty, many districts have established mentor teacher programs for probationary teachers. By pairing an effective veteran teacher with new faculty members, a very useful, collegial relationship can develop. These mentor teachers should undergo special training for their role and be given release time as well as extra compensation. Such a program can not only help new teachers with their work in the classroom but also can aid them in their relationships within the district. Even if a district has a mentor program, the principals cannot divorce themselves from the professional development of their faculty.

Well-planned staff development opportunities for teachers can make a positive difference in a school. Unfortunately, what has passed for ongoing teacher training has often been ineffective. A typical approach in the past might have included two or three superintendent or staff development days per year. Such a day would begin with a welcome by the superintendent, followed by an "inspirational" keynote speaker and then a group of unrelated workshops. Even if there was a specific theme for the day, there was often little or no follow-up to the information that was provided. There also seems in many cases to be no direct relationship between the programs and what the teachers are actually doing in the classroom. Another traditional approach has been the financial encouragement for teachers to take additional graduate courses. Again, the problem has been that too often the courses were ones that had little to do with improving instruction in the classroom. In many cases, neither the one-day conference nor the graduate course approach is directly tied to the school district's overall objectives.

In an article entitled "The Old Model of Staff Development Survives in a World Where Everything Else Has Changed," Edward Miller reports that:

> Research over the last twenty years has consistently shown that teachers learn new methods best not from lectures by experts but by seeing those methods used in actual classrooms, by designing their own learning expe-

riences, by trying out new techniques and getting feedback on their efforts, and by observing and talking with fellow teachers (see "Schools
Where Teachers Learn," *HEL*, July 1986).[3]

There is help for principals seeking to develop effective staff development programs for their faculty. Linda Darling-Hammond and Mil-
brey McLaughlin have suggested the following goals:

- Redesign school structures to support teacher learning and collaboration around serious attention to practice;
- Rethink schedules and staffing patterns to create blocks of time for
teachers to plan and work together;
- Organize the school into small, collaborative groups;
- Make it possible for teachers to think in terms of shared problems,
not "my classroom" or "my subject";
- Consider using peer review rather than standard hierarchical supervision; and
- Include everyone in a school community, such as principals, counselors, and parents, in creating a shared purpose.[4]

Even with an effective professional development plan in place, principals are going to encounter faculty members who are unhappy.
Michael Weber has made several suggestions concerning this inevitable
problem. First of all, an administrator must understand that there are
negative people in most organizations and that they will only change
when they are able and willing to change themselves. Such changes are
most likely to happen in a building where there is a positive climate. Weber argues that an environment that includes a principal who is a positive role model and sensitive to the concerns of others is more likely to
help even the constant critics to become more positive. He also suggests
that a school in which the faculty and staff can laugh together will make
a difference.[5]

People feel better about their work when their accomplishments are
recognized. A schoolwide bulletin that features teachers and staff who
have made a noteworthy accomplishment is helpful in maintaining good
morale. Frequent positive notes from the principal that are also placed
in the personnel file are also appreciated. One school district instituted

a very popular practice for parents and students. Teachers could share with the principal when a student did some type of outstanding work. That evening the principal would make a "happy call" to the parents. When a parent first knew that the principal was on the line, the initial thought was that there must be a problem. To receive good news was always a pleasant surprise for the entire family.

When a faculty or staff member is going through a difficult time in his or her personal life, such as a death of a family member, principals should demonstrate their concern. Too many administrators fail to recognize the importance of attending the calling hours or the funeral when a faculty member loses a loved one. Deaths and births are significant events in anyone's life and an employer should be a source of comfort rather than concern during these times. At the same time an administrator is showing compassion for faculty and staff members, it is impossible to totally separate the fact that principals are responsible for supervision and evaluation of school employees.

It is sometimes difficult to be both a mentor and an evaluator. The reality is that most teachers see the principal primarily as the boss who will be evaluating their performance. This is especially true with nontenured faculty. A classroom observation by the principal can be a very stressful event for teachers. Even though this is true, it is not impossible for a principal to also be a mentor for faculty members. It is important that teachers understand that principals do want them to succeed. This is especially true for instructors whom the principal helped to hire. The first time an administrator observes a teacher's class can set the tone for the relationship. During the follow-up conference that occurs, principals should attempt to help teachers to feel comfortable about talking about the lesson observed, as well as other aspects of their work in the building. When a class goes poorly, the principal should still find some positive comments about the faculty member's work in the school. If this first private conversation can cause teachers to see the principal as a person who truly wants to help, some of the tension will be lifted for subsequent observations.

Nothing will make observations a painless process for faculty, and there will be times when the principal has to be honest and straightforward in describing a teacher's weaknesses. Mary Jo McGrath has written that

For many in education, the words "accountability," "supervision," and "evaluation" are frightening. They imply having one's feet held to the fire for failure. These processes exist in a paradigm of fear and dread. Educators blame others and blame the circumstances for their lack of effectiveness rather than taking personal responsibility.

This phenomenon in human dynamics should not be seen as unique to teachers and administrators in education. It exists everywhere. We all have a tough time taking and giving criticism. We all have that very common fear of failure.[6]

Despite the fact that most educational professionals will admit that there is a significant percentage of less-than-adequate teachers in our schools, most teachers are given positive annual evaluations. McGrath goes on to ask:

Why don't supervisors say it like it is? The repercussions are simply too great and the immediate benefits too small. Consider the lost working relationships, excessive time pursuing a plan of improvement and the tiny return on the investment given what it takes to remove one permanent teacher through the evaluation system. It is easier to pick your battles, give satisfactory ratings to all and work off the record with those teachers with whom you think you can make a difference.[7]

The fact is that administrators must be trained to become effective in the area of teacher evaluation. If a principal was not well prepared in graduate school for this function or during an internship, it is essential to seek help in this crucial job task.

Effective classroom evaluation and an ongoing staff development program are two of the ways that schools can cope with the ever-present challenge of retaining the best teachers in the profession. Currently, about one-third (or 250,000) of teachers per year are quitting the profession during their first three years. Schools with a large number of minority students seem to have the biggest problem. Jim Hunt, speaking for the National Commission on Teaching and America's Future, has written that in order to solve the problem of retention, "we should have been focusing on improving working conditions in the school, having greater career opportunities for teachers, having the right pay for them, showing the right kind of appreciation."[8] Schools are made less effective when large numbers of faculty members turn over each year. Almost more than any other single factor, a principal's positive leadership in a school building can help to retain good teachers.

One of the ways this can be accomplished is to support teachers in their efforts to maintain student discipline. Lack of support by an administrator is one of the most frequently heard criticisms of principals and assistant principals. A teacher whose student is sent to the office for disrupting a class does not want to see that child coming back from the office smiling five minutes later. Teachers would prefer that students have some fear of being sent to the office, as this is one of their ultimate weapons as they attempt to affect students' behavior. A principal who is seen as being hesitant to punish or afraid of critical parents will quickly lose the respect of the faculty and staff. Currently, administrators are being held accountable for the number of out-of-school suspensions in their building. The information often appears in statistical reports that are made public. Some faculty and staff believe that principals have become overly sensitive about being accused of suspending too many students, even when a student is deserving of such a severe penalty. One teacher is quoted as saying that:

> I am retiring this June because it is so frustrating. They put all of these pressures on you in the classroom to teach, but when you have an unruly child—and not just talking out, I mean students who prevent learning—they do nothing to help you.
>
> What affects the levying of administrative suspensions? Ms. Solomon notes that these punishments show up in statistical profiles of a school in the local press. She also believes that William Moore, the M.S. 202 principal, and other principals have been reluctant to crack down on serious misbehavior for fear that too many administrative suspensions will lead the Department of Education to lower the principals' scores on new official evaluations, the first of which were sent out to some principals two weeks ago.[9]

Sometimes, principals are also forced to discipline teachers and staff. Unfortunately, school employees sometimes fail to conform to school policies and expected behaviors. One area that is currently a problem for some school administrators is the clothing teachers choose to wear to work. As a result of some criticisms of teacher attire, a number of districts have attempted to develop a dress code for their faculty. A typical teacher reaction to such a policy was quoted in a local newspaper, "A highly restrictive dress code is seen as harassment. A teacher needs the freedom to create his or her most effective style."[10] Many administrators and board of education members view teacher dress as "a projection of image and an element of classroom control."[11] On the other hand, "teachers may see any push to regulate their behavior as an infringement of their civil rights."[12] The only way to deal with this kind of issue, as well as similar problems, is to attempt to work with the employees to develop a policy that is acceptable to the majority. The recent movement toward site-based management has established an arena for dealing with such problems in many schools.

In dealing with faculty and staff where site-based management is a reality, a principal faces a significant leadership challenge. In areas where a principal is dominant, it is possible that a committee could now become divisive. Dealing with a group of teachers, parents, and possibly students in reaching a consensus can be complicated and time consuming. *The Harvard Education Letter* published an issue with the headline, "Shared Decision-Making by Itself Doesn't Make for Better Decisions." Under the title, the following statement is included, "A study of high schools finds that democracy in governance helps teachers 'buy in' to reform, but real change depends on the principal's vision and leadership."[13] Although principals may not always act as chairs of building-level committees, they still are essential as advisors and facilitators. A study by Carol Weiss concluded that:

> If shared decision making is to engage teachers in basic change. . . it has to be seen as a permanent part of the school's structure and be supported with time, money, training, and symbolic endorsement from the district level on down. Unless teachers become convinced that it is permanent and authentic and that they really hold power, they are unlikely to take collective steps toward reform.[14]

Working with building-level committees is only one of the ways that principals interact with faculty and staff. A more formalized relationship has developed between the building administrator and employee

unions. It is inevitable that there will be times when the interests of a
union and the principal will come into conflict. Despite this realization,
principals should attempt to develop a strong working relationship with
union leaders, especially those who represent the union in their building. If union leaders can learn to respect a principal's integrity, the problems that are faced are more likely to be resolved without a major conflict. Some interesting experiments are demonstrating how unions and
the school district can work together. One such example is where the
teacher union has agreed to help with "marginal teachers." Such "intervention strategies" occur when the union and the district agree that a
teacher is in need of additional mentoring. Several cities have replicated
an intervention model first established in Toledo, Ohio. After significant
debates, Cincinnati and Columbus (Ohio), as well as Rochester (New
York), New York City, and Seattle have begun their own programs.[15]

There is also a realization in some areas that unions have gained too
much influence in our schools. A bill introduced in the Massachusetts
legislature would strip unions of some of their powers.

> Gone would be the unions' powers to control everything from teacher-
> evaluation standards to school dismissal times, supporters predict.
> - The bill would give district school administrators the same manage-
>   ment flexibility enjoyed by increasingly popular charter schools.
> - Principals would regain control over such basic questions as how
>   much of the day is spent on English instruction, how long students
>   are in class, whether teachers serve cafeteria duty, and how teachers
>   are evaluated.
> - The unions, however, would still negotiate salaries and benefits.
> - The new chairman of the Massachusetts Board of Education ob-
>   serves that the legislature "is looking for ways to show its indepen-
>   dence" from teachers unions—and adds that "influence has its lim-
>   its."[16]

Teacher unions are likely not to be the only employee groups that
have formed unions. In many districts, all of the employees in a building might be members of one union or another. As a result, the principal may need to be concerned about enforcing and living with contracts
that have been negotiated by the custodians, the cafeteria workers, and
sometimes the secretaries. Even when such employees are not union-

ized, they might report to another supervisor in the district. The building custodians and cleaners might be directly supervised by the superintendent of buildings and grounds, while the bus drivers report to the director of transportation. When this is the organizational pattern of a district, a principal must develop a working understanding with these other administrators. When the principal wants a building custodian to fix a broken window, it may be necessary to first contact the superintendent of buildings and grounds. The annual reviews of the work of the custodians, bus drivers, and cafeteria workers are likely to be done by someone other than the building principal. Still, it is important for the individual responsible for the management of the building to have sufficient authority with everyone who works in the school to ensure that all of the necessary functions are carried out. Because of some often complicated organizational patterns within a district, this can only be done if principals demonstrate sensitivity and care in their relationships with staff members. It is very possible that other supervisors in the district may be very protective of their personal authority and view a principal who to them appears heavy handed as uncooperative.

Another complication that is increasingly occurring in schools is that some staff are not even directly employed by the school district. A number of districts have decided to hire contractors for such services as student transportation and school lunches. A few are even contracting out their maintenance and cleaning functions. When a district signs a formal agreement with a private company to provide a service, the principal has even less authority in supervising these employees. Although the building administrator may be responsible for disciplinary incidents on a school bus, the driver, who might be part of the problem, is an employee of the company providing the service. In such cases, the school has a contact person with the company. Theoretically, any service provider is likely to want to satisfy the customer in order to ensure that the contract will be renewed. This can and often does result in a positive working relationship between the school administrator and the company. Unfortunately, there are also times when there are problems with contract companies. Because the business is responsible for hiring, firing, and training its own employees, many principals would prefer the added control they might have when their staff members are directly employed by the school district.

The factors discussed in this chapter affect principals' relationships with their faculty and staff. Even so, there are building administrators throughout the nation whose personal qualities and leadership styles have gained for them the respect of those who work in their school. Such support is still not enough to guarantee a principal's success. Developing positive relationships with parents and the community is also essential.

NOTES

1. National Commission on Teaching and America's Future, "What Matters Most: Teaching for America's Future," *National Center on Teaching and America's Future Publications*, at www.tc.edu/nctaf/publications/whatmattersmost .html (accessed 1 February 2003).

2. "What Qualities Do Principals Look For in a New Teacher?" *Education World*, 1998, at www.education-world.com/a_admin/admin071.shtml (accessed 1 February 2003).

3. Edward Miller, "The Old Model of Staff Development Survives in a World Where Everything Else Has Changed," *Harvard Education Letter* 6, no. 1 (January/February 1995): 1.

4. Anne C. Lewis, "A New Consensus Emerges on the Characteristics of Good Professional Development," *Harvard Education Letter* 8, no. 3 (May/June 1997): 3.

5. Michael R. Weber, "Coping with Malcontents," *American Association of School Administrators*, 2003, at www.aasa.org/publications/sa/2003_02/ weber.htm (accessed 21 February 2003).

6. Mary Jo. McGrath, "The Human Dynamics of Personnel Evaluation," *American Association of School Administrators*, 2000, at www.aasa.org/ publications/sa/2000_10/McGrath.htm (accessed 21 February 2003).

7. McGrath, "The Human Dynamics of Personal Evaluation."

8. "Report: Teacher retention biggest school woe," *CNN.com*, 29 January 2003, at www.cnn.com/2003/EDUCATION/01/29/teacher.shortage.ap/index/ html (accessed 20 February 2003).

9. Jim O'Grady, "Soft on Students Means Hard on Us, Teachers Say," *New York Times*, 12 January 2003, at www.nytimes.com/2003/01/12/nyregion/12teac .html?pagewanted=print&position=top (accessed 14 January 2003).

10. Ruth E. Sternberg, "Attending to Teacher Attire," *American Association of School Administrators*, February 2003, at www.aasa.org/publications/sa/ 2003_02/sternberg.htm (accessed 21 February 2003).

11. Sternberg, "Attending to Teacher Attire."

12. Sternberg, "Attending to Teacher Attire."

13. Edward Miller, "Shared Decision-Making by Itself Doesn't Make for Better Decisions," *The Harvard Education Letter* 6, no. 6 (November/December 1996): 1–4.

14. Miller, "Shared Decision-Making."

15. Lisa Birk, "Intervention: A Few Teachers' Unions Take the Lead in Policing Their Own," *Harvard Education Letter* 5, no. 6 (November/December 1994): 1–4.

16. National Center for Policy Analysis, "Principals Given More Power in Massachusetts," *National Center For Policy Analysis Idea House*, 2001, at www.ncpa.org/~ncpa/pi/edu/pd041999d.html (accessed 1 February 2003).

8

THE PRINCIPAL'S RELATIONSHIP WITH PARENTS AND THE COMMUNITY

Building principals are frequently very visible in their communities, especially in smaller school districts. This is especially true for the parents of the children in the principal's school. As a building administrator, there are several reasons for principals to foster parental participation in the work of the school. "Researchers and practitioners have long acknowledged a strong link between parent involvement and children's success in school. Studies conducted over the last thirty years have identified a relationship between parent involvement and increased student achievement, enhanced self-esteem, improved behavior, and better school attendance."[1]

There are a number of factors that can inhibit parental involvement. One of the major problems is that parents today frequently have busy and hectic lifestyles. Single parents particularly find it difficult in that they are attempting to support their children with a full-time job and still find time to participate in school activities. Even children living with two parents who are both working have very crowded schedules. Parents come home at night tired and have to decide the best way to spend their few leisure hours. Very often, they choose not to give up precious time at home for a PTA meeting or to participate in a school advisory committee.

In many communities, there are other barriers to parental involvement—especially in urban areas where teachers and principals come from educational, socioeconomic, and racial backgrounds different from the parents. In such districts, poor and minority parents are sometimes hesitant to interact with predominantly white school professionals. To some parents, the teachers and administrators are the "education experts." There are also the problems of lack of child care and transportation, which in many cases limit the ability of parents to become active in their children's school.[2]

To deal with such obstacles, schools must go out of their way to make parents and community members feel welcome. Anyone who answers the telephone in a school or acts as a receptionist must be sensitive and helpful to everyone who seeks information or help. In the name of efficiency, many schools have installed sophisticated telephone answering programs to guide calls to the correct individual. Too often, these systems can be frustrating to callers, especially if they are not sure who they need to speak with to solve a problem. A single, pleasant, and well-informed operator who can steer calls to the correct people can be more welcoming for anyone who calls the schools. It is important that telephoning the school not become a complicated and unpleasant experience.

The office secretaries are the first individuals that people meet when they come to a principal's office. Just as the receptionist in a doctor's or lawyer's office creates a helpful and welcoming atmosphere, those who greet people in an administrator's office can affect how visitors feel about the school and possibly even the principal. Successful administrators are very aware of the need to create a warm and friendly environment for visitors to the school. Several examples of some administrators' thoughts on this issue suggest the importance of creating a welcoming environment in a school office.

"Customer service is near and dear to my heart," says Glenn Hughes, whose Georgia school has a parent volunteer greet each visitor with a smile and "Welcome to Stowers School!" Hughes never hesitates to handle phone calls himself: "My voice on the phone reinforces my belief to parents that everyone at Stowers is here to serve."

Florida's Sue Colton is "never afraid to apologize to a parent if they've had a bad experience." Alabama's Terry Beasley: "Parents must feel that they are genuinely heard, valued, and an essential part of our school. If so, they will be our best advocates; if not, our worst nemesis." Colorado's John Youngquist has his school provide foreign-language assistance for parents.

"I tell my staff that the public gets only one chance at a first impression," says Vicki Wallace, in Tennessee. "So our grounds are in good shape, our building is clean, the front office is full of smiles and it's never empty."[3]

Schools can also be helpful to parents of preschool children. At Roscoe Elementary School, located in the San Fernando Valley, an educational program called "Mommy and Me" has been very successful. The weekly class for mothers with preschool children provides:

> a chance to learn some English, get to know other parents, and familiarize their toddlers with group activities. The class is also just one of many educational opportunities open to parents at the school and throughout the Los Angeles unified system's District B. . . .
>
> Bernardo Madera, who has a 3rd grader at Roscoe, is participating in the Mommy and Me class with her 3-year-old daughter. She says it helps her as a mother and prepares her younger daughter for preschool. "She's not going to cry like most of the kids," Madera predicts. "And I have learned how to be social."[4]

Parents who have a special interest are often eager to organize as a group. One problem that has united parents in a number of districts is the problem known as attention deficit hyperactivity disorder (ADHD).

> "ADHD is not just a school-day disorder; it is an all-day disorder," said Harold S. Koplewicz, M.D., director of the New York University Child Study Center. "In addition to its proven impact on academic performance, ADHD also affects how children get along with family and friends, complete homework assignments, and participate in after-school activities. Successful management of this condition needs to address all aspects of a young person's daily life."[5]

Schools can help parents of children with this disorder by sponsoring programs featuring physicians and psychologists who can help parents understand the problem. Both parents and teachers can be invited to these information meetings. Although it is not officially designated as a handicapping condition requiring a formal individualized education program, it is mutually beneficial for parents and teachers of children with ADHD to work together. Sometimes these parents will form their own organization and invite school officials to participate.

Undoubtedly, secondary schools will have several groups of parents who are seeking to promote specific programs. A very common group in many districts is the sports booster club. Although such an organization can make valuable contributions to the interscholastic athletic program, it can also at times become overly involved in the management of the program. Both the secondary principal and the district athletic director should stay close to such an organization. If the membership begins to become critical of a coach, it can lead to a difficult situation for the administration. There is also the potential that the group will lobby aggressively for additional funds for athletics in the school budget.

Another area that might also have its own booster club is the music department. They too can become active in budgetary matters. Parents who favor a gifted and talented program, or who become watchdogs of the special education program, can also present a challenge to the building principal. As the building manager, a principal must listen carefully to any parent group, even though it will be impossible to satisfy all of them.

For many districts, the primary parental organization is the Parent Teacher Association. Principals should attempt to be actively involved with the building chapter of this organization. It is important to urge teachers to also attend the meetings and to participate in the activities of the group. Some schools have very active and powerful parent organizations, while in other buildings they do not exist. Principals can act as a member of the executive committee of such a group and help to plan the programs. PTA meetings provide an excellent opportunity for spotlighting school programs. This can include performing groups, outside speakers, or presentations by faculty members.

The school's PTA sometimes can help principals establish volunteer programs in their school. Volunteers can include parents as well as other individuals from the community. Senior citizens can also be targeted to assist in the building. Bringing older citizens to school can be helpful in raising their level of support for school budgets and bond issues. It is also possible for elementary schools to arrange for senior high school students to help out. A Future Teachers of America Club will often assist in setting up volunteer opportunities for students interested in the teaching profession.

Individuals willing to help out in school can be used to assist teachers, librarians, and office workers. To be effective, principals should ensure that the program is well planned and monitored. The following factors should be kept in mind:

- A volunteer program should have a specific person assigned to administer the recruitment, training, and assessment of all volunteers.
- All potential volunteers must be interviewed and screened to determine their strengths and weaknesses. Acceptable placement of volunteers depends upon a careful assessment of each individual.
- There must be a planned program of orientation and training for all volunteers.
- There should be a performance assessment process in place. On rare occasions, it will be necessary to discontinue the service of a volunteer for being undependable or displaying inappropriate behavior.
- There should be a plan for regularly recognizing the work of volunteers. A volunteer appreciation dinner would be an appropriate time for awarding certificates to recognize the many hours that volunteers have spent working in the school.
- Especially for senior citizens, a volunteer program might consider providing transportation for volunteers.[6]

Volunteer programs are just one way schools can benefit from working with community members.

The number of school–community partnerships nationwide is soaring as school leaders capitalize on the potential benefits that can be gleaned from bringing schools, parents, and community agencies together to help students learn. Their goal: to develop "community," "full-service" or "extended-service" schools that deliver not only educational excellence, but also a menu of social services tailored to the needs of individual communities. . . .

Some examples:

- The Missoula County, Mont., school district has teamed up with a number of partners, including the local United Way and the Western Montana Mental Health Clinic, to develop initiatives designed to help students at risk of doing poorly in school become responsible and productive citizens. Specifically, the collaborative effort has provided the schools with mental health services, family resource centers, on-site child care, bullying prevention, and community service programs and mentoring. Teachers and administrators report that the students involved in the programs the longest are demonstrating the biggest improvement in attitude and behavior.
- In Tukwila, Wash., a social worker from the county's Department of Social and Health Services has worked for years out of a local school in order to be more accessible to the students and families she serves. Also operating out of the schools are counselors employed by several nonprofit community-based agencies. Other partnerships provide students with on-site tutoring and parents with Saturday morning training programs. School district data reveal that as such services increase, so do student test scores.
- An extended school-day program in Central Falls, R.I., provides after-school, weekend, and summer programs specifically designed to boost academic achievement. The effort was the result of myriad collaborations with small, local agencies, such as the local chapters of the YMCA and Boy Scouts, several Hispanic social service agencies, and the City of Central Falls.[7]

In recent years there has also been a dramatic increase in programs involving cooperation between schools and the business community. Such alliances have sprung up in rural, suburban, and urban areas. "Private funding for public K–12 schools is the most rapidly growing philanthropic sector, according to Howard Schaeffer of the Public Education Network (PEN). . . . How fast this trend is growing is hard to gauge, Schaeffer says, in part because there are thousands of groups that raise less than the $25,000 threshold for IRS reporting, but its impact is unmistakable."[8]

One of the most impressive of these organizations is the Alliance for Education, established in Seattle, Washington. With a budget of more than $13 million, and a full-time staff of twenty, this organization provides the Seattle School District with programs to develop leadership teams, train potential principals, and numerous other initiatives that assist schools. Businesses such as Microsoft provide funds, along with a major fundraiser event each year by the organization.

Business educational cooperative organizations also provide mentor programs for students, sponsor career days, and contribute equipment to schools. Community businesspeople have a strong interest in the quality of schools in their community. Companies that require skilled workers in their organization need to be able to claim a strong school system. Unless the commercial interests in a district become involved and supportive of school programs, it is very possible that individual representatives of business, as well as business organizations, can become critics of the school system. Because businesses (and their owners) are most often significant property taxpayers, they can be less than supportive if they feel that the school system is inefficient and ineffective.

Business involvement in schools can also create some interesting dilemmas for school principals. Soft drink and candy companies are often willing to share profits with a school for the privilege of placing their vending machines in a building. For districts with limited budgets, such inducements are tempting. To agree to such an arrangement might be popular with most students, but some parents, teachers, and cafeteria workers might actively protest. Principals should be extremely careful about agreeing to such arrangements in their buildings.

Along with businesses in the community, other groups can be helpful to schools. An organization called Making Connections is building cooperative endeavors "at the neighborhood level between schools, churches, and health care agencies in twenty-two communities around the country."[9] This type of cooperative program will only occur if the school administrator is supportive and takes a leadership role. On the other hand, it is not necessary that the principal do all of the work. In a report published by the Charles Stewart Mott Foundation, it is suggested that principals should find "others to help manage the initiative" by developing "a partnership with another organization, a guest/host relationship in your school. . . . In other words, you don't have to do it all. With parents, and other members of the community, form an advisory board for your program."[10]

In finding organizations to work with, administrators should also consider various government agencies. Police departments offer Drug Abuse Resistance Education (DARE) programs to help students deal with peer pressures involving drugs and alcohol. Fire departments are usually available for presentations on fire safety. It is extremely helpful for school counselors and psychologists, as well as principals, to have open communication with the social workers and probation officers who are working with their students.

Although principals must be cautious about stepping across the line separating church and state, church youth leaders and clergy can also assist schools in working with students. During a crisis, such as the death of a student, clergy can assist as counselors. Principals will also be involved in making decisions concerning religious activities in school or on school grounds. Currently, prayer groups meeting before school at an activity called "See You at the Pole" are one way that students are allowed to pray collectively before school. The courts have also ruled that Bible studies can be held after school as long as other groups in the community are allowed to use the school facilities. Faculty and staff members are allowed to be present during these gatherings, but not to actively participate. The courts have also ruled that local churches must be given a limited amount of school time for release-time religious education when it is requested. These classes cannot occur within the school building, and teachers cannot introduce new work to their class during this allotted time. Churches often hold individual or collective baccalaureate services for the senior class. It is important for principals to develop a cooperative attitude with churches and parochial schools within the district. A "church and state fight" can be extremely disruptive in any community.

Developing positive relationships with all community groups, including parents, should be a high priority for all school administrators. Today's school districts are heavily engaged in the field of public relations. Some districts and individual schools do quite well in this area, but others have a lot to learn. In an article entitled "How to Market Your School System without Making Mistakes," Susan Rovezzi Carroll and David J. Carroll offer the following advice:

- Don't assign public relations solely to a single person or department. Marketing is everyone's responsibility. Individual employees should be encouraged to submit ideas for stories in the school newsletter or for newspapers or other media.

- Individuals who have the primary responsibility for marketing or public relations should be appropriately trained.
- Schools should consider communicating with a number of different constituencies and should develop several different ways to distribute information about the school.[11]

Finding ways to have positive stories about the school on local radio and television can be extremely helpful in improving the image of the school. Publicizing a school event, project, or a student achievement not only reflects well upon the school but is also appreciated by students and parents. Too often, the media only concentrates on schools when there is a problem. On the other hand, principals cannot expect journalists to cover events unless they have ample prior notice.

Another way to highlight the activities of a school is to offer performances of music groups to local organizations. Having students perform at the senior citizen's center or even at nursing homes can only enhance the district's image in the community. Art shows made up of student work at all grade levels can be featured at a local mall or a municipal building.

In recent years, districts have begun developing their own websites to communicate with their communities. If the appropriate expertise is not available on the faculty or staff, community members can be helpful in establishing and maintaining a school website. Increasingly, this has become a method for informing the community about upcoming school programs. Parents considering moving to the area are also checking out school district websites.

One caution for school administrators is in order. Administrators at every level tend to feature themselves in every newsletter and press release. Perhaps most guilty of this practice are college presidents, whose picture often is featured three or four times in a single publication. The only newsletters that are more self-centered are those of elected officials. Students and teachers should be highlighted in communications to the community.

Another concern is the tendency of educators to use professional jargon in dealing with the public. It is not helpful or appreciated when communications are laden with terms like authentic assessment, adaptive technology, the affective domain, and anchored instruction. Clearly written and factual prose should be the rule. It is also important that communications not be perceived totally as a public relations campaign, but rather as a truthful and fair source of information about school programs.

In all of these efforts, the principal is a key figure. Especially in smaller districts, principals will be actively involved in marketing and public relations. They will be asked to be speakers at meetings of service organizations and church groups. Especially for secondary principals, they will be in the public eye at school events several times each week. For all building administrators, attendance at school concerts, plays, and PTA meetings is expected. Students appreciate seeing their principal at various sporting events. Although it is impossible for an administrator to attend every contest, an effort should be made to see each team perform at least once in a season. Aside from the need to evaluate the athletic programs, the participants appreciate the principal's presence, and it also gives an administrator something to talk with students about. Despite the fact that a principal might especially enjoy basketball, for example, he or she should not ignore the wrestling and swimming teams. Parents are also aware of an administrator's support or lack of support of an activity.

As the leader of the school, principals are expected to be visible and involved members of the community. This is most true in poor, rural districts where the building administrator can be among the best-paid individuals in a school district. There will be pressure to be involved in charity campaigns and to join civic organizations. Participation in this type of activity can be very time consuming. As a result, it is essential that administrators carefully plan their schedules and develop priorities for the use of their time.

Working with parents and representatives of the community is important, but it is only one of the crucial roles played by a building principal. A part of the job that has grown increasingly more important is that of the principal's responsibility to maintain a safe and orderly building. This important subject is the topic of the next chapter.

NOTES

1. Karen Mapp, "Making the Connection between Families and Schools," *Harvard Education Letter* 8, no. 5 (Sept./Oct. 1997): 1–3.

2. Mapp, "Making the Connection."

3. June Million, "Treat All Parents Right," *Education Digest* 67, no. 4 (December 2001): 37–38.

4. Linda Jacobson, "Parental Guidance," *Teacher Magazine* 14, no. 5 (February 2003): 7–8.

5. "ADHD Not Just a School-Day Disorder: New Survey Reveals All-Day Impact of ADHD on Children and Their Parents," *KidSource Online*, 2002, at www.kidsource.com/health/all.day.adhd.html (accessed 1 February 2003).

6. Brian O. Brent, "What You Never Knew about School Volunteers," *Education Digest* 66, no. 2 (October 2000): 55, as published in William Hayes, *So You Want to Be a School Board Member?* (Lanham, Md.: Scarecrow Press, 2001), 128–29.

7. Priscilla Pardini, "School Community Partnering," *American Association of School Administrators*, 2001, at www.aasa.org/publications/sa/2001_08/pardini1.htm (accessed 21 February 2003).

8. Andreae Downs, "Buying Quality," *Harvard Education Letter* 19, no. 3 (May/June 2003): 8.

9. Pardini, "School Community Partnering."

10. National Association of Elementary School Principals, "Working Well Together: School Community Initiatives," *Communicator*, 1999, at www.naesp.org/comm/c0399.htm (accessed 21 February 2003).

11. Susan Rovezzi Carroll and David J. Carroll, "How to Market Your School System without Making Mistakes," *ICP Online*, 2002, at www.icponline.org/feature_articles/f15_02.htm (accessed 1 February 2003).

MAINTAINING A
SAFE AND ORDERLY BUILDING

The success or failure of principals has most often been judged by their ability to maintain a well-disciplined building that has a safe and orderly environment for students and teachers. Today, many people are convinced that our public schools are characterized by violence and that they are possibly dangerous places. The notion that schools have become more disorderly and students less disciplined has also been with us for some time.

A local teacher's organization, in an attempt to convince the public that the challenges of teachers have increased dramatically, published the following in a local publication.

How Times Have Changed:
"Are We Still Addressing the Issues of the '40s?"
The top seven discipline problems in public schools in 1940 and the top seventeen problems in 1990s.

1940
1. Talking
2. Chewing gum
3. Making noise
4. Running in the halls
5. Getting out of turn in line
6. Wearing improper clothing
7. Not putting paper in wastebaskets

1990

1. Drug abuse	10. Extortion
2. Bombings	11. Robbery
3. Alcohol abuse	12. Gang warfare
4. Murder	13. Assault
5. Pregnancy	14. Abortion
6. Absenteeism	15. Burglary
7. Suicide	16. Arson
8. Vandalism	17. Venereal disease[1]
9. Rape	

Although school discipline has always been an issue, the concern for a student's safety in school has emerged more recently. Especially since the incident at Columbine High School and the more recent attack on September 11, 2001, worries about school safety have been significantly heightened. Schools in rural and suburban communities have joined those in urban areas in hiring security guards, installing closed-circuit cameras, and utilizing metal detectors. New regulations requiring name tags, searching book bags, and lockdown drills have become commonplace. The "war on terrorism" has added various-colored alert codes to which schools are expected to react. Emergency plans have become mandatory for schools in many states. One result is that more families are looking to the alternative of home schooling in recent years, in part because of their concern for the safety of the public schools. New and tougher discipline policies have been introduced in many districts.

Building principals are also faced with what appears to be an increase in the areas that create student behavior and discipline problems. The Josephson Institute (2000) published a report card entitled "The Ethics of American Youth." Over 15,800 students were surveyed. A few of the findings of this report helped paint a picture of our current middle school and high school students.

1. Although 27 percent of middle schoolers and 31 percent of high schoolers say they think it is sometimes OK to hit or threaten a person who makes them angry, about 70 percent have actually hit a person in anger at least once in the past year. . . . As might be expected, boys are considerably more likely to have permissive attitudes about violence. Compared to girls, more than twice as many

high school boys think it is OK to hit or threaten others. Still, 61 percent of high school girls admit that they have hit someone in anger at least once in the past year.

2. More than one in five high school boys (21 percent) and 15 percent of the middle school boys said they took a weapon to school in the past year. . . . Boys are much more likely to carry weapons than girls.

3. Nearly one in three middle school boys (31 percent) and 60 percent of the high school boys said they could get a gun if they wanted to. . . . It is especially discomforting that middle school students who admitted they had been drunk in school at least once in the past year were nearly three times more likely to have access to weapons than their classmates—59 percent versus 22 percent. Similarly, 71 percent of the high schoolers who said they had been drunk at school in the past year had access to a gun, far higher than the overall high school rate of 47 percent.

4. Drugs are available to most high school students. . . . Drug access and usage is similar among boys and girls though slightly higher among boys.

5. Nearly 10 percent of the middle school boys and 20 percent of the high school boys say they have been drunk at school at least once in the past twelve months. Girls are less likely to engage in this behavior.

6. More than one in three students say they don't feel safe at school. Generally, boys are more fearful of school than girls.[2]

Fear of violence is one of the main reasons students feel unsafe in school. A study of bullying in middle schools done by Sandra Harris and Garth Petrie reported that 92 percent of the students surveyed had observed some sort of bullying at least "sometime." Nearly 50 percent of students admitted that they failed to notify anyone about the incident. The primary reason given for not reporting the problem was the student's perception that 60 percent of the teachers and 70 percent of the administrators were not interested in dealing with this type of issue.[3]

Along with the problem of bullying, school disciplinarians are also concerned about fights between students. Fights in school and on school grounds are not a new phenomenon. Unfortunately, confrontations today might be considered more serious than ever when one realizes the fact that so many students are bringing weapons to school. "In a recent Gallup Poll, citizens were asked what they thought were the biggest problems for public schools and communities, and the number one answer was fighting/violence/gangs (15 percent). The second most common response was lack of discipline (14 percent)."[4] School administrators are sometimes called upon to break up student fights. Authorities suggest that the first step is to give a loud and clear verbal command in the hope that it will have an effect. If students remain physically engaged, it is often helpful to seek the help of another adult who might be nearby and certainly it would be appropriate to ask a student to summon a male teacher. Physical intervention requires that any adult use "reasonable" force to separate the antagonists.[5] It is important that once the students are separated they are sent to different rooms to ensure a cooling-off period before mediation can even be attempted.

For the principal, fighting in school is an offense that requires appropriate punishment. Some schools have developed policies that ban any type of fighting and require that all participants be given the same penalty. This will often include an out-of-school suspension. The trouble with such a blanket policy is that frequently one student is more responsible for the fight than the other. In rare cases, one of the students is merely defending himself or herself against an attack. The story behind every fight is different. Disciplinarians encounter cases where a shove or angry words by one student leads to another student being hospitalized. There may even be cases where assault charges are appropriate. Unless the principal is an effective mediator, any fight starting in school can continue at a different venue. Perhaps the most serious are those involving gangs of students. A conflict between school athletes and a group of kids wearing black jackets can create a major crisis for the school administration. Fighting between girls can be an especially fierce and troubling event.

As a result of the current concern over violence in schools, many districts have rewritten discipline policies to include more serious consequences for inappropriate behavior. The most talked about approach has been labeled the Zero Tolerance Policy. This is an idea that first surfaced in the 1980s in the fight against illegal drugs, and was further encouraged by the Safe and Drug-Free Schools and Communities Act, passed by Congress in 1994. This law requires the expulsion of students who bring drugs or weapons into a school building. In some districts, the zero tolerance approach has been expanded to "include harassment, fighting, gang activity, toy weapons, any drugs, threats of violence, and hate offenses."[6]

Even though the public strongly supports strict penalties for inappropriate behavior in schools, principals have found themselves in difficulty as they attempt to enforce these new policies.

> Recently, zero tolerance was again thrown into the national spotlight when six high school students from Decatur, Illinois, were expelled for brawling. Immediately, the print, broadcast, and Internet editorialists rehashed every news-making zero tolerance incident—children suspended or expelled for bringing nail clippers or mouthwash to school, for scribbling threats or scary messages, for writing horror stories. . . .
>
> Ironically, almost no news reports praised schools for their safety efforts. Little was heard of how many dangerous incidents at schools had been avoided, or whether students felt safer as a result of these get-tough policies. Instead, schools were accused of taking the easy way out, hiding behind their rules, and using a one-size-fits-all approach to discipline. Papers were full of phrases like "draconian punishment" and "zero tolerance, zero sense." Accusations that school authorities "ignored the needs of these troubled youth" or that schools were "scared stupid" surfaced on TV and in syndicated columns.[7]

As a result of the sometimes-negative publicity of zero tolerance policies, other approaches have been introduced. Many districts have developed "alternative schools" for students in trouble. "The Department of Education says the number of schools for students who break the rules has ballooned from 2,606 in the 1993–94 academic year to 4,818 in 2000–01."[8] These schools attempt to

> combine individual attention with stringent academic standards and an insistence on personal responsibility. Students must sign a contract stipulating that they will behave.
>
> Mujeres y Hombres Nobles, the oldest alternative high school for troubled kids in Los Angeles County, has been a model around the country. It serves 75 students, mostly Latinos from nearby East L.A. Their infractions range from truancy to firearm possession, drug selling and sexual assault.

There are no window bars, security guards, metal detectors, or pat downs at the front door—just a friendly receptionist and a big, brightly colored bulletin board welcoming all visitors. "If we installed security devices, we'd be telling our kids that we don't trust them," says Cathleen Corella, the principal, who proudly reports that there have been just five fights at the school in 10 years.[9]

This approach raises a number of difficult questions for a school district. For instance, there is the issue of whether students who do well in an alternative school can, with good behavior, return to a regular program. Some of the students who are candidates for one of these schools might also be designated as special education students. There is the question of whether some alternate education programs are a proper placement for special education students. In some districts, families of children assigned to alternative classrooms are actually challenging the placements in court. In Philadelphia, a class action suit has been filed to overturn a 2002 state law designated to improve school safety. This law created the alternative programs. Still, there are claims of success and signs that, if the programs are carefully conceived and administered, they can make a positive difference.

Both of the national principals' organizations have supported federal legislation "that would require states and school districts to provide alternate educational services, supervision, and counseling for a student who is expelled."[10] The groups also recommend that policies address the following:

- Consideration should be given for age and grade level
- The punishment should fit the "crime"
- Educational services should never stop[11]

Even when a principal has a zero-tolerance policy and the possibility of assigning students to alternative education programs, student behavior problems will not disappear. Many districts have chosen to introduce into their schools a "school resource officer." "Part teacher and part law enforcer, SROs give schools a valued presence that can deter students from causing trouble."[12]

After the incident at Columbine High School, Congress passed a program entitled COPS in Schools, which provides significant amounts of financial aid to place police officers in school buildings. Actually, the idea has been around since the 1960s, but the practice began to grow dramatically in the 1990s. Individuals chosen for this special duty need to be carefully selected and receive special training. There is also a trend to encourage school resource officers to engage in projects designed to prevent violence.[13]

Another way some communities are looking to improve the security in their buildings is through environmental design.

> The physical environment can dramatically affect feelings, behavior, and the way in which we view others. It also can affect the safety and perceived safety of those who use the environment. Conscientious design, appropriate use, and good maintenance of properties can promote positive social interaction, orderly behavior, and increased perceptions of safety. These assertions are the basis of an evolving body of knowledge and public-safety initiatives referred to as Crime Prevention through Environmental Design (CPTED).[14]

Several examples of the ways that architects can assist in creating a safe environment are as follows:

- *Natural surveillance*. This is design and placement of physical features in such a way as to maximize visibility. These features include windows, walkways, assembly areas, corridors, stairways, doors, and lighting. The objective is to provide an environment in which you can see and be seen, to eliminate hiding or hard-to-see places, and thereby increase the perception of a human presence. For instance, in choosing landscape material, schools should make sure that the material provides benefit without blocking views.
- *Access management*. This is the physical guidance of people coming and going from a space. Examples include the judicious placement of signage, entrances, exits, fencing, landscaping, lighting, and other way finding elements, such as the use of color, to provide orientation and direction. The objectives of access management are to keep people on safe routes, enhance emergency response, decrease the sense of being lost, avoid conflicts, and prevent trespassing.

- *Territoriality.* This is the use of physical attributes that delineate space and express ownership. Attributes include art, displays, signage, landscaping, fencing, and pavement treatments. Also, buildings and other features can be placed so they create a perceived area of influence, similar to the concept of circling the wagons. The objectives are to increase the sense of pride and ownership felt by the students, faculty, and school personnel, and put others on alert that they are coming into territory that is owned and cared for. This gives the message that unacceptable behavior will not be tolerated.[15]

Perhaps the most significant educational legislation passed by the Congress in recent years is the No Child Left Behind Act. This law addresses the issue of school safety, and it will affect the efforts of principals to maintain well-disciplined schools. One of the most far-reaching clauses in the bill states "that any students attending a 'persistently dangerous public school' have the option to transfer to a 'safe' public school. It takes effect at the start of 2003–04 school year, as does a related NCLB mandate requiring the choice option for students who have been victims of a 'violent criminal offense while in or on the grounds of a public school they attend.'"[16]

States must draft policies that allow for this version of "school choice" for students who feel unsafe. If a school is labeled as "persistently dangerous, the district must notify parents; offer all students the opportunity to transfer to a safe public school within the district, including a public charter school; develop a corrective action plan; and implement the plan in a timely manner. According to the guidelines, 'transfers of students generally should occur within 30 school days.'"[17]

As a result of pressure from both the federal government and state governments, school districts are busy developing strategic plans for dealing with school violence. New companies and consultants are available to help in this effort. One of the most popular approaches is to invest in high-tech security equipment. There are new developments in surveillance cameras and access via the web to local police departments. The cameras have sound alarms when certain behaviors are detected. For example, the camera might set off an alarm if a fight were to occur. A nontoxic aerosol spray is now available for helping to detect illegal drugs. Many school buses are equipped with video cameras to record student misbehavior on a bus. The use of digital cameras has become popular, and new face scanners are being developed that will identify students in a crowd. Another company has devised a doorway weapon detector, which can identify a weapon carried by students as they approach the building. Other schools have installed swipe card detectors to monitor those coming in and leaving the building.[18]

Although many students report that these high-tech security measures make them feel safer, the equipment is expensive. As a result, school boards must choose between attempting to provide security and traditional budget items, such as new books for their library. Such decisions are being made by building principals. In order to make the appropriate choices, school managers might need to call upon specialists who can offer technical assistance. Many schools are going beyond metal detectors and security guards in developing their safety plans. They are looking for ways to deal with some of the root causes of student violence. Programs in conflict resolution and peer mediation have been introduced.[19] Also teachers and school employees are being trained in violence prevention methods. In New York State there is a requirement that anyone applying for teacher certification must first participate in a special training program called Students Against Violence Everywhere (SAVE). The training includes warning signs of potential violent behavior, various steps necessary for schools to create a safe learning environment, and ways to create a safe and nurturing learning environment for students in the classroom.

The safety plans of most districts now include provisions for what are called lockdowns. This practice received national attention with the recent sniper attacks in the Washington, D.C., area. Students were kept inside the building and sometimes in one classroom all day. Gym classes, recess, and all outside activities were curtailed. In Fairfax County, a full-scale lockdown now entails not drawing the blinds and restricting all movement in the building. Even though such plans are being made, a survey of safety experts found that 55 percent of the plans they evaluated were inadequate and 52 percent had never been tested.[20]

In an effort to make schools safer, principals are attending seminars and school committees are working with the police and community groups all over the country. What is becoming increasingly clear is that schools need the help of the entire community. School employees, parents, community agencies, and even students can help to devise practical and realistic methods for improving conditions in our schools. This will probably not happen without the leadership and the active participation of principals. It is the principal who is likely to organize meetings involving the police and other governmental agencies, along with parents, to discuss appropriate policies for the school. In an article published in *Education Digest*, the following suggestions were made:

- Include a cross-section of the community in developing school safety plans.
- Develop programs that seek to deal with the causes of student violence.
- Have an ongoing program of training and staff development for school employees.[21]

Most authorities urge students to become actively involved in efforts to stem school violence. It goes without saying that young people are reluctant to report questionable behavior by their peers. If schools are going to attempt to encourage students to become whistle-blowers, it is essential that students who speak to authorities about potential problems be protected. Nevada State Senator Valerie Wiener was quoted as saying, "These children who come forward aren't looking for rewards; they're looking for safety. Safety for their loved ones, themselves, and their careers."[22] Beyond that, Bill Alexander, in an article entitled "Protecting Students Who Inform on School Violence," suggests that we should be praising students who come forward to prevent violence. In the same article, Alexander quotes educational law professor Robert DeKoven, who cites the following incidents where student information has made a difference:

- Several students informed on a student who brought eighteen bombs, a sawed-off shotgun, and a loaded pistol to a high school in Elmira, New York. The whistle-blowers were commended.
- In Ft. Collins, Colorado, alarmed students told school officials about classmates who planned to reenact the Columbine massacre at their high school. The whistle-blowers were commended.
- In Hoyt, Kansas, a tipster called a hotline for warnings about school violence, leading to the arrest of students with a cache of weapons.[23]

Student violence issues such as these are not confined to the United States. An incident in Germany ended in sixteen deaths, compared to the fifteen students who lost their lives at Columbine. Still, authorities in Europe have been less active in their responses, perhaps because European countries have much stricter gun control legislation.[24]

The availability of guns is a reality that American communities and schools will continue to grapple with. There is little doubt that this and other security issues will continue to be a major concern for school principals. It is up to the principal to create the kind of environment in which students feel secure. Writing in a book entitled *The Great School Debate*, Harold Howe II suggested that:

> The personality and style of a principal can contribute immensely to a school's atmosphere, but there is no single prescription for how a principal should behave. I have known both highly directive and somewhat authoritarian principals, who managed to create an atmosphere that students and teachers found comfortable, and others who placed their emphasis on participation and group process. Probably the main ingredient is integrity and fairness in dealing with others.[25]

Books have been written and classes have been taught on how best to manage students' behavior. One of the most respected authors in this field is William Glasser. Glasser's work has been included in numerous textbooks and has influenced many school administrators. C. M. Charles summarized Glasser's current ideas as follows:

1. All of our behavior is our best attempt to control ourselves to meet our needs.
2. We always choose to do what is most satisfying to us at the time.
3. All of us have inborn needs that we continually attempt to satisfy. Included among those inborn needs are:
   a. to belong
   b. to gain power
   c. to be free
   d. to have fun
4. We feel pleasure when these needs are met, and frustration when they are not.
5. We feel a continual urge to act when any need is unsatisfied.

6. If schools are to have good discipline, they must create classes in which fewer students and teachers are frustrated.

7. Only a discipline program that is concerned with classroom satisfaction will work. That means that students must feel they belong, have some power, have a sense of freedom, and have fun in learning.[26]

In his book *The Quality School*, Glasser "claims that we must stop settling for minimal goals such as reducing dropouts and discipline problems and start convincing students to work hard because there is quality both in what they are asked to do and how they are asked to do it. Right now few students work hard and almost none do what we or they call quality schoolwork."[27] He goes on to suggest:

> that we replace the "bossing" that turns students and staff into adversaries with a system of management that brings them together. He claims that when we stop pushing students to increase their scores on state assessment tests that mean nothing to them and start teaching in a way that satisfies their needs, discipline problems will disappear and every student will find satisfaction in doing well in school.[28]

Another expert who was especially influential in the 1980s is Lee Canter, who developed a program called Assertive Discipline. For Canter, the key to discipline is "catching students being good: recognizing and supporting them when they behave appropriately and letting them know you like it, day in and day out."[29] His method calls for teachers to develop and post in their classroom a minimum number of rules. Also posted would be the consequences for disobeying these rules. These consequences would be listed in order of their severity. A first offense might merely mean a check on the blackboard next to the student's name. For the second incident, the student might receive ten minutes in the "time-out" place in the classroom. The third offense might mean a call home or a trip to the principal's office. The teacher would also post a sign with rewards for positive behavior. These could include group rewards such as a party or individual gestures such as a positive call to parents. Teachers adopting Canter's methods most likely would do so in cooperation with the principal, as often the final consequence of behavior would be discipline by the principal.[30]

Whether it is the theories of William Glasser, the approach of Lee Canter, or any of a number of other student management plans, school principals will be judged by the faculty, the community, and the students on the effectiveness of behavior management in their buildings. Any principal who does not take this role with utmost seriousness is bound to fail. Even those school leaders who are effective in this area will not necessarily succeed. Especially today, the principal will also be judged by his or her effectiveness as an instructional leader in the school.

NOTES

1. "How Time Have Changed," *Warsaw Penny Saver*, 12 February 1992.

2. Josephson Institute of Ethics, "The Ethics of American Youth—Violence and Substance Abuse: Data and Commentary," *2000 Report Card: Report #1*, 2 April 2001, at www.josephsoninstitute.org/Survey2000/violence2000-commentary.htm (accessed 1 February 2003).

3. Sandra Harris and Garth Petrie, "A Study of Bullying in the Middle School," *National Association of Secondary School Principals* 86, no. 633, at www.nassp.org/news/study_bullying_1202.html (accessed 20 February 2003).

4. Lynette Fields, "Handling Student Fights," *Clearing House* 75, no.6 (July/August 2002): 324–26.

5. Fields, "Handling Student Fights."

6. Gerald N. Tirozzi and Vincent L. Ferrandino, "Zero Tolerance: A Win-Lose Policy," *National Association of Secondary School Principals*, at www.nassp.org/publicaffairs/views/zero_tol.htm (accessed 1 February 2003).

7. Tirozzi and Ferrandino, "Zero Tolerance."

8. Sonja Steptoe, "Taking the Alternate Route," *Time* 161, no. 2 (13 January 2003): 50–51.

9. Steptoe, "Taking the Alternate Route."

10. Tirozzi and Ferrandino, "Zero Tolerance."

11. Tirozzi and Ferrandino, "Zero Tolerance."

12. Mike Kennedy, "Teachers with a Badge," *American School and University* 73, no. 6 (February 2001): 36–37.

13. Kennedy, "Teachers with a Badge."

14. Sherry P. Carter and Stanley L. Carter, "Planning Safer Schools," *American School and University* 73, no. 12 (August 2001): 168–70.

15. Carter and Carter, "Planning Safer Schools."

16. Ellie Ashford, "The Dangerous Schools 'No Child Left Behind,'" *Education Digest* 68, no. 5 (January 2003): 12–15.

17. Ashford, "The Dangerous Schools."

18. Ellie Ashford, "High-Tech and the Human Touch for Safer Schools," *Education Digest* 68, no. 2 (October 2002): 49–53.

19. Teresa L. Kramer, Kim A. Jones, Joann Kirchner, Terri L. Miller, and Crystal Wilson, "Addressing Personnel Concerns about School Violence through Education, Assessment, and Strategic Planning," *Education* 123, no. 2 (Winter 2002): 292–304.

20. Sean Cavanagh, "Sniper Attacks Prompt District 'Lockdowns,'" *Education Week* 22, no. 7 (22 October 2002): 11–12.

21. Ann Marie C. Lenhardt and Jeanette H. Willert, "Linking ALL Stakeholders to Stem School Violence," *Education Digest* 68, no. 1 (September 2002): 37–44.

22. Bill Alexander, "Protecting Students Who Inform on School Violence," *Education Digest* 67, no. 8 (April 2002): 10–14.

23. Alexander, "Protecting Students Who Inform."

24. Darcia Harris Bowman, "Across the Atlantic, Europeans Take Different Approach to School Safety," *Education Week* 21, no.37 (22 May 2002): 1–2.

25. Harold Howe II, "Giving Equity a Chance in the Excellence Game," in *The Great School Debate*, edited by Beatrice Gross and Ronald Gross, 291–92 (New York: Simon & Schuster, 1985).

26. C. M. Charles, *Building Classroom Discipline: From Models to Practice* (New York: Longman, 1989): 126–27

27. William Glasser, *The Quality School: Managing Students without Coercion* (New York: Harper Collins, 1992): back cover.

28. Glasser, *The Quality School.*

29. Arthea J. S. Reed, Verna E. Bergemann, and Mary W. Olson, *In the Classroom: An Introduction to Education* (Boston: McGraw Hill, 1998): 332.

30. Reed, Bergemann, and Olson, *In the Classroom.*

10

THE PRINCIPAL
AS AN INSTRUCTIONAL LEADER

The idea that the principal must be an effective instructional leader within a school district emerged in the 1980s as a result of several research studies. These studies showed clearly that when the building administrator led initiatives to improve instruction, the achievement levels of children were higher. By the early 1990s, there was more in the literature about the need for "school-based management" and "facilitative leadership."[1] More recently, educational journals have again included articles about the instructional role of principals but with a somewhat different focus.

For Richard DuFour, a veteran school administrator, the past emphasis was wrong.

Eventually, after years as a principal, I realized that even though my efforts had been well intentioned—and even though I had devoted countless hours each school year to those efforts—I had been focusing on the wrong questions. I had focused on the questions, What are the teachers teaching? And How can I help them to teach it more effectively? Instead, my efforts should have been driven by the questions, To what extent are the students learning the intended outcomes of each course? and What steps can I take to give both students and teachers the additional time and support they need to improve learning?[2]

The author goes on to argue that principals should change their goal of seeking to be an instructional leader to becoming a "lead learner." As an instructional leader, principals focused on teacher observations, modeling teaching styles, introducing instructional innovations, and presiding over endless curriculum meetings. DuFour and others are suggesting that building administrators be primarily concerned with developing a school that is a "learning community." To do so, principals must foster a building culture conducive to continual student learning and professional growth for faculty and staff.[3]

The National Association of Elementary Principals, in a report written in 2001, highlighted the idea that "effective principals lead schools in a way that places student and adult learning at the center. . . . Traditionally, principals have managed schools and overseen budgets, buildings, staff members, and students."[4] The report recommends that even though a principal must remain a school manager, many of these tasks can and should be delegated to others. In building a school learning community, the elementary principals' organization makes the following suggestions:

- Principals must learn to balance management and instructional roles;
- Principals must set challenging academic standards that demand rigorous content and excellent instructional methods;
- Principals must foster adult as well as student learning;
- Principals must be familiar with and utilize current research; and
- Principals should engage parents and other community groups.[5]

In considering the goal of creating learning communities for children as well as adults, there are several ways in which a principal can play a significant role. First, the leader must have a vision of what such a school might be like. A vision is only helpful if one has the ability to articulate to others the type of environment that is being sought. In carrying on conversations with faculty and staff, it is essential that a principal be able to speak intelligently about curriculum standards, how students learn, teaching methods, and assessment tools. Faculty members can quickly ascertain if a principal knows what he or she is talking about. As an intellectual leader of a school, the administrator must join with the faculty in an ongoing effort to remain involved in learning about the field. Money should be set aside for a professional library, and educational periodicals should be made readily available to all faculty members.

Some principals actually lead early morning or after-school book discussion groups. An important book is chosen and read by the principals and volunteer faculty. Each week, the group comes together to discuss a portion of the book. In-service training for faculty is a responsibility of the school district, but principals will be key in ensuring that these activities actually contribute to helping a school reach its objectives. The following have been identified as characteristics of an effective professional development program:

- Has the goal of improving students' learning
- Helps teachers meet the future needs of students who learn in different ways and who come from diverse backgrounds
- Provides adequate time for inquiry, reflection, and mentoring, and is an important part of the normal working day of all educators
- Is rigorous, sustained, and adequate to the long-term change of practice
- Is directed toward teachers' intellectual development and leadership
- Fosters a deepening of subject-matter knowledge, understanding of learning, and appreciation of students' needs
- Is designed and directed by teachers, incorporates the best principles of adult learning, and involves shared decisions
- Balances individual priorities with school and district needs
- Makes best use of new technologies
- Is site-based and supports a clear vision for students[6]

Staff development is an essential aspect to any school's attempt to increase student learning. Among our students, there is a strong feeling that schools can do a better job. Only 25 percent of the students surveyed in a large research project done by MetLife strongly agreed that teachers in their school have high expectations for all students. Only 23 percent of students describe their classes as being "very challenging." The percentage of principals and teachers who feel that we have high expectations and challenging courses is significantly higher.[7]

Statistics such as these, as well as massive evidence highlighting the poor showing of U.S. students in comparison to other nations, provide a strong argument for change in our schools. Even with this need to improve instructional outcomes, principals of many of our schools continue to be "managers of bureaucracies, not leaders of school reform."[8] Barbara Newfeld of Education Matters suggests that districts need to do the following in order to bring about change in their schools:

- Develop and support teams of teachers who work together;
- Show the school how to set goals and plan effective strategies;
- Make the school a place where teachers have the freedom and the support they need to find the best ways to teach;
- Take a measure of the progress of reform.[9]

For Michael Fullan, the roles of "change leaders" in schools and in business are similar. "Like a business leader, the principal of the future—the Cultural Change Principal—must be attuned to the big picture, a sophisticated conceptual thinker who transforms the organization through people and teams."[10] In addition, such leaders should have moral purpose, the ability to understand change, skill in developing and improving relationships within the organization, ability to lead in knowledge creation and sharing, and finally, skill in creating a coherent instructional program.[11] The author offers the following guidelines for understanding change:

- The goal is not to innovate the most. Innovating selectively with coherence is better.
- Having the best ideas is not enough. Leaders help others assess and find collective meaning and commitment to new ways.
- Appreciate the implementation dip. Leaders can't avoid the inevitable early difficulties of trying something new. They should know, for example, that no matter how much they plan for the change, the first six months or so of implementation will be bumpy.
- Redefine resistance. Successful leaders don't mind when naysayers rock the boat. In fact, doubters sometimes have important points. Leaders look for ways to address those concerns.

- Reculturing is the name of the game. Much change is structural and superficial. Transforming culture—changing what people in the organization value and how they work together to accomplish it—leads to deep, lasting change.
- Never a checklist, always complexity. There is no step-by-step shortcut to transformation; it involves the hard, day-to-day work of reculturing.[12]

The challenge of bringing about change in a school can be overwhelming for a principal. First, leaders must realize that they cannot change an organization alone. Roland Barth, a former principal and current consultant on principal development, wrote "All too many principals fall into the trap of playing the all-knowing one."[13] Others have written about the essence of changing an organization.

> California State University Professor, Linda Lambert, argues that "leadership is about learning together, and constructing meaning and knowledge collectively and collaboratively." . . . Richard Elmore offers a more succinct definition of school leadership: "Leadership is the guidance and direction of instructional improvement. . . . Distributed leadership in which formal leaders widely distribute leadership responsibilities among various role groups in the organization while they work hard at . . . creating a common culture, or set of values, symbols, and rituals.[14]

How does one learn to be this type of leader? A report published by the Council of Chief State School Officers attempts to define a quality program for preparing instructional leaders. The document identifies the following characteristics of such a program:

- A quality program will validate teaching and learning as the central activities of the school.
- A quality program will engage school leaders in well-planned, integrated, career-long learning to improve student achievement.
- A quality program will promote collaboration to achieve organization roles, while meeting individual needs.
- A quality program will model effective learning processes.
- A quality program will incorporate measures of accountability that direct attention to valued learning outcomes.[15]

Washington, D.C., is undoubtedly a city in need of educational change. In attempting to bring this about, the school district is focusing on giving special training to its building principals. New building administrators are required to participate in a two-year program focusing on instructional improvement. Superintendent Paul L. Vance, on assuming his position in Washington, observed that principals were merely "business managers; they were community outreach advisors," and they were "running six different union contracts . . . but they were not instructional leaders."[16] Unlike many programs, the experiences designed in Washington included summer workshops away from the principal's building along with follow-up activities that were held in the school between September and June. The goal is to make the training "job embedded," "long term," and to ensure that "it engages teachers, because you can't just have the principal interested in this stuff."[17]

For most principals, bringing about instructional change emphasizes increasing students' language art skills. Without improving reading and writing skills, it is unlikely that students will show growth in other academic areas. Elementary principals especially must become experts in this important curriculum area. Douglas Fischer, Nancy Frey, and Douglas Williams have identified "seven literacy strategies that work." A building administrator should be conversant in these widely used techniques, which are supported by research.

1. *Read-alouds*—The idea is that teachers read to their students for at least five minutes every day to help ensure that students frequently hear fluent reading.
2. *K-W-L Charts*—These language charts start with the question, "What do you know about the topic?" Following this discussion, students are asked, "What do you still want to know about the topic?" Once the unit of study has been completed, the language charts are used again and students answer the third question, "What did you learn about the topic?"
3. *Graphic Organizers*—Graphic organizers provide students with visual information that complements the class discussion or text; for example, a science teacher placed a number of magnetic strips with terms on them related to the concept of matter on a board at random. The teacher invited individuals to come to the board to

create a graphic representation of the information they had been studying. He also asked that they draw lines and write in the relationships between the words.

4. *Vocabulary Instructions*—Students are given exercises in word families, prefixes, suffixes, word roots, vocabulary journals, and word sorts.

5. *Writing to Learn*—Teachers conclude their classes by asking for a summary of what students have learned in class, for a description of one highlight of the class, or a prediction of what the class would study the next day.

6. *Structured Note Taking*—The students draw a vertical line about two inches from the left side of the paper, log main ideas and key words to the left and details to the right of the line, and write a brief summary of the lesson at the bottom of the page.

7. *Reciprocal Teaching*—Reciprocal teaching allows students to become the instructors of the content they are studying. Working in groups of four, the students read a text passage together—followed by a protocol for predicting, questioning, clarifying, and summarizing, skills that teachers have modeled over a series of lessons until students are comfortable assuming these assigned roles. In a physical education class, for example, the teacher introduced the rules of volleyball by providing students with a text that explained all the rules of the game. He could have explained the rules verbally, but he knew that reading, asking questions, and clarifying the rules in small groups would both foster literacy skills and increase the students' understanding of the game.[18]

Whether it is in a physical education class or an English class, student learning can be improved in a school where the principal is actively involved in the academic program. Perhaps one of the most useful summaries of the qualities of a successful, instructional leader is found in a book written by Steven J. Gross entitled *Staying Centered: Curriculum Leadership in a Turbulent Era*. He identifies the following characteristics:

1. *Experienced but still growing*. The experiences of successful curriculum leaders most often included work as classroom teachers. In addition, they knew the setting they were working in, and they

saw themselves as people who were growing and evolving. Although they had considerable experience, they were not tied to the status quo.

2. *Centered on students and families.* Those curriculum leaders making a positive difference in their districts were focused on student learning. Any innovation was measured by its potential success in helping children and families.

3. *Willingness to experiment but not reckless.* Leaders often insisted on a tryout period for new ideas. There also was a willingness to take the necessary time required to prepare people for change. Districts planning major changes do not begin in April to change their high school to block scheduling in September.

4. *Highly engaged but not overwhelmed.* One leader described the goal as "taking the work but not yourself seriously." Despite interruptions and setbacks, the leaders maintained the vision for the group and kept them on track. At the same time, they did not appear fanatical or driven.

5. *Trusting but not naïve.* Leaders gave trust and thus received it from colleagues. At the same time, they did not harbor unrealistic expectations for others. The leaders understood that those participating in the group attempting to bring about change had other priorities and concerns. As a result, the leaders let the process unfold without pushing too hard.

6. *Powerful but not overbearing.* The group must feel that they have support from the top but not domination by a dictator.

7. *Visible but quiet.* The leader must continually show enthusiasm and actively participate in the process, but it is not necessary to be a person who talks more than others. Informal contacts with teachers and students were used to encourage the process.

8. *Dignified but informed.* As a leader, it is important to strike the appropriate balance between informality and serious purpose. It is essential that leaders be willing to laugh and have fun with the group but at the same time maintain a level of formality that signifies the seriousness of the task.

9. *Demanding but understanding.* Although patient, leaders expect high levels of performance. If a subcommittee is assigned to explore a certain aspect of the program being considered, the

leader must make it clear that the group must do a thorough job on its assignment. If the superintendent is chairing a group, it is important that agendas and minutes are always prepared. Everything about the process should be professional, but if a person or group occasionally falls short, the leader must not embarrass or humiliate group members.

10. *Highly ambitious but for their group, not themselves.* The leader in curriculum change must do everything possible to help the group feel strongly about the goals being pursued. Teachers should be encouraged to attend conferences and make visitations to other schools. The willingness of leaders to expend district funds on individual members of the team emphasizes the importance each individual has to the project. The goals must be shared, and not just those of the leader.[19]

Along with these characteristics, there is one additional element that is undoubtedly essential. Robert Evans begins his essay entitled *The Authentic Leader* with these words:

> Transformation begins with trust. Trust is the essential link between leader and led, vital to people's job satisfaction and loyalty, vital to followership. It is doubly important when organizations are seeking rapid improvement, which requires exceptional effort and competence, and doubly again to organizations like schools that offer few extrinsic motivators (money, status, power). And it is as fragile as it is precious; once damaged, it is nearly impossible to repair. When we have come to distrust people, either because they have lied to us or deceived us or let us down too often, we tend to stay suspicious of them, resisting their influence and discounting efforts they may make to reform themselves.[20]

Trust will only be given to one who is seen as having integrity. Thorndike uses the following words to describe integrity: "Honesty, sincerity, and uprightness."[21] When one is seen as having these qualities, it helps to create respect, a quality that is necessary for any leader. Even though these qualities are crucial, they are only part of the essential qualities of any leader. In order to move an organization forward, a person must have a clear and mature vision for what an effective school should be. Along with vision, a principal must have the appropriate political skills. Such skills include the ability to communicate in a one-on-one situation, with smaller groups, or addressing a large audience. An essential ability of a political leader is to be a good listener who can use and benefit from the ideas of others. Perhaps the most important leadership ability is to be able to bring together people with divergent views and help them reach an acceptable consensus. Too often, when one talks about political skills, there is a negative connotation. The fact is that for any organization that relies, even in part, on collective decision making, the leader must be a good politician.

Finally, an instructional leader must not be perceived as a person lacking human qualities such as humility and a sense of humor. Others will appreciate persons who can laugh, especially at themselves. Consideration of all of these qualities can be overwhelming for someone thinking about being a principal. No one can be strong in every one of these areas. It would be wrong to conclude that being an effective instructional leader in a school is a goal that will be unobtainable. The fact is that in every state there are successful schools that are being led by effective principals. These are schools where continuous improvement is part of the culture. It is being done and, therefore, it is not an impossible task; still, it would be less than candid to suggest that being an effective instructional leader is not difficult given the multitude of issues facing principals in the twenty-first century. It is the purpose of the next chapter to identify some of these pressing problems that will be facing building administrators in the days ahead.

NOTES

1. Larry Lashway, "Developing Instructional Leaders," *ERIC Digest*, 2002, at http://eric.uoregon.edu/publications/digests/digest160.html (accessed 21 February 2003).

2. Richard DuFour, "The Learning Centered Principal," *Educational Leadership* 59, no. 8 (May 2002): 12–15.

3. DuFour, "The Learning Centered Principal."

4. Mark Stricherz, "Elementary Principals' Group Calls for Focus on Leading Instruction," *Education Week* 21, no. 10 (7 November 2001): 17–21.

5. Stricherz, "Elementary Principals."

6. Judith Renyi, "Building Learning into the Teaching Job," *Educational Leadership* 5 (February 1998): 72, as published in William Hayes, *So You Want to Be a Superintendent?* (Lanham, Md.: Scarecrow Press, 2001), 86.

7. Ken Schroeder, "Education News in Brief," *The Education Digest* 67, no.4 (December 2001): 71–73.

8. "What Principals Need to Lead School Reform," *Reforming Middle Schools and School Systems*, at www.middleweb.com/SRC2iii5.html (accessed 24 February 2003).

9. "What Principals Need to Lead School Reform."

10. Michael Fullan, "The Change Leader," *Educational Leadership* 59, no. 8 (May 2002): 16–20.

11. Fullan, "The Change Leader."

12. Fullan, "The Change Leader."

13. "Learning to Lead, Leading to Learn," *NSDC*, at www.nscd.org/leader_report.html (accessed 1 February 2003).

14. "Learning to Lead, Leading to Learn."

15. "Learning to Lead, Leading to Learn."

16. Mark Stricherz, "D.C. Principals' Training Designed to Boost Instructional Leadership," *Education Week* 21, no. 2 (12 September 2001): 6–7.

17. Stricherz, "D.C. Principals."

18. Douglas Fisher, Nancy Frey, and Douglas Williams, "Seven Literacy Strategies That Work," *Educational Leadership* 60, no. 3 (November 2002): 70–73.

19. Steven J. Gross, *Staying Centered: Curriculum Leadership in a Turbulent Era* (Alexandria, Va.: Association for Supervision and Curriculum Development, 1998), 11–12, as published in William Hayes, *So You Want to Be a Superintendent?* (Lanham, Md.: Scarecrow Press, 2001), 83–84.

20. Robert Evans, "The Authentic Leader," in *The Jossey-Bass Reader on Educational Leadership*, introduction by Michael Fullan (San Francisco, Calif.: Jossey-Bass, 2000), 287–308.

21. E. L. Thorndike and Clarence L. Barnhart, *Thorndike Barnhart Intermediate Dictionary*, 2nd ed. (Glenview, Ill.: Scott, Foresman, 1974), 445.

II

CURRENT ISSUES FACING PRINCIPALS

To a large extent, the emphasis on the role of principals as instructional leaders has occurred because of a national trend requiring school accountability as measured primarily by the results of so-called high-stakes tests. The *New York Times* carried the following headline on January 9, 2003: "Amid Criticism, Bush Promises to Produce Education Gains."[1] From Washington, as well as from most state capitals, new programs are being introduced to help raise test scores.

Noting the trend, the National Association of Secondary School Principals issued a statement on high-stakes testing. In it, they deplore relying on a single test as the sole criterion for assessing student learning. The result of this practice, they suggest, is narrowing the curriculum and causing teachers to merely teach to the test. The statement is especially critical of using tests as a way to determine whether a student can graduate, for grade advancement, or for rewarding or punishing teachers, principals, schools, districts, and even states. The organization urges that assessment decisions be based on the following principles:

- Testing must be viewed in context as one tool among a variety required to gauge academic progress. Use of single test scores often presents an inaccurate picture of academic progress.

- Quality testing assessments are diagnostic in nature and designed to show how well students apply knowledge.
- Accurate comparisons of test scores to determine progress are based on the scores of the same student cohort groups across test dates as opposed to the scores of the same grade level of students from test date to test date. In addition, variables such as mobility rates and dropout rates are taken into account.[2]

The report goes on to make the following recommendations related to testing:

- Tests should be diagnostic in order to provide educators with the necessary information to positively affect the teaching and learning of each student.
- Tests should be designed in a variety of formats and provide opportunities for students being tested to demonstrate a range of abilities.
- Adequate resources must be provided to ensure that reliable testing methods and assessments are instituted, and which are aligned with clearly articulated standards of learning.
- Adequate resources must be focused on providing remedial assistance to students and to schools for the purposes of improving teaching and leadership strategies with regard to testing and assessment. Sufficient amounts of time must be allowed to determine whether these strategies are effective.
- Students who fall behind, at any point, in the K–12 continuum must be immediately identified—through ongoing, reliable, and diagnostic assessments—and provided additional support and assistance. The use of trained tutors, after-school programs, and mandated summer schools should be incorporated into a school's plan of action.[3]

Other critics of the trend have also been outspoken in expressing their concern about the tendency to rely too heavily on tests. James Popham, in an article published in the *School Administrator*, wrote, "Unfortunately, many educators' current efforts to succeed in this accountability-induced contest are causing serious educational harm to students. Today's evaluation of schoolwide performance based on students' standardized test scores must be ended."[4] Although the reliance on tests has, to a large extent, been brought about by pressure from politicians and state boards of education, Popham blames professional educators in schools and colleges for letting it happen. He writes that, "Our apathy has allowed this mismeasurement of educational quality to flourish and led to a situation that has placed teachers and administrators in an untenable position. Even worse are the adverse educational consequences for our students."[5]

Another concern is that high-stakes testing greatly inhibits teacher and student creativity in the classroom.[6] Because large amounts of time are spent on reviewing for tests, there are those teachers who have canceled field trips, student projects, and cooperative education exercises in order to have sufficient time to review for the examination. There is now a backlash movement that is touting the need for alternative assessment. These methods include student portfolios, skills tests, and required presentations. Just as educators have long urged varied teaching methods to accommodate multiple intelligences and varied learning styles, many feel that there must also be a number of assessment methods to measure student learning.

An additional negative result of the heavy reliance on tests is cheating by students, teachers, and administrators. In an article in the *New York Times*, Alfie Kohn blamed the enormous pressure on educators to produce better results for the wave of cheating that has occurred in New York City, as well as in other school districts. Along with the major scandal in New York, principals and teachers have been accused of cheating in Texas, Kentucky, Rhode Island, and Connecticut. According to Robert Schaeffer, director for the National Center for Fair and Open Testing, "In today's environment, this type of thing [cheating] will continue. . . . When test scores are all that matter, teachers, principals, and students will get their results by hook or by crook. When their job or future depend on one thing, people do unethical, irrational, and illegal things."[7]

For principals, there is another important duty related to high-stakes testing. As the manager of the school, they are expected to ensure the tests are appropriately administered and graded. If something goes wrong during the testing process, it will be the principal who will be held responsible.

Finally, as our society becomes more and more concerned about keeping schools accountable based on the results of tests, as a nation, we cannot ignore the inequality that has emerged in our schools. We have traditionally relied upon our local communities to finance and manage schools. During the second half of the nineteenth century and the first half of the twentieth century, states took on more and more responsibility for public education. State financial aid now provides approximately the same amount of money for schools as does local taxes. The formulas that determine state aid were originally meant to give more assistance to districts with low property bases so that there would be at least some semblance of equality among the schools of the state. In part because of the political strength of the suburbs, the goal of equal opportunity, as determined by per pupil expenditures, is not being achieved in many areas of the country. As a result of the system's heavy reliance on local property tax, our more affluent suburban districts are currently spending double or triple the amount per student as rural and urban communities do. For example, in New York State, the Midstate School Finance Consortium published a poster with the heading, "Unfortunately Some Kids Just Don't Get It." On the poster were pictures of four fifth-grade students in different schools in New York State. Under one picture, it showed Gabriela, from Nyack, New York, who was receiving an education costing $9,851.00 per year. Nyack is a suburb of New York City in Rockland County. Hannah attends Sherburne-Earlville, a small, rural district in upstate New York. Her district is spending $4,973.00 per student. A student from Niagara Falls, New York, a small city with numerous educational problems, is receiving an education costing the district $7,291.00. Finally, Jacob, from Port Jefferson on Long Island, is lucky enough to be in a district that is spending $16,668.00 per child.[8]

The level of financial support is just one factor that affects the ability of schools to provide a quality education. Districts with high levels of poverty and a large number of non-English-speaking students have special problems. These schools are at a great disadvantage when their testing results are compared with districts containing primarily students from culturally advantaged homes.

Despite all of the factors that might mitigate against the use of high-stakes tests to ensure that schools are accountable, there is no question that most schools can do a better job. The Nation at Risk report, published in 1983, publicly highlighted how poorly our students were doing on standardized tests compared to their counterparts in other countries. It was difficult to argue in the 1980s that schools could not be improved. A reform trend swept the nation, which found states and individual districts developing initiatives to raise standards and to expect more from our students. This was especially true of the approximately 13 percent of our children who had been classified as being in need of special education. Thus the so-called inclusion movement for special education students saw schools being expected to challenge *all* students to meet higher expectations. At the same time, the national government and the state governments were eagerly developing educational standards that articulated what students should know and be able to do.

Developing specific educational objectives and standards was widely accepted as a necessary process to bring about higher academic achievement. In any case, the practice of developing these standards led to what appeared to be the necessary next step of assessing whether students were meeting the standards. It has been difficult during this period of reform for professional educators to argue against testing and accountability given the public perception that schools were failing. The business community has been very instrumental in supporting the goal of developing standards and means of ensuring that schools are accountable. These same business leaders would also go the next step in suggesting that schools not meeting the standards after attempting some remediation should be penalized and perhaps even closed. Many politicians have agreed with those in the business community who have said that schools must measure up.

However much school administrators might be uncomfortable with what they feel are unrealistic expectations, they cannot deny the need to seek "continuous improvement" in our schools. As schools attempted to meet these higher expectations, a number of methods have emerged. During the nineties, one of the most widespread initiatives has been the effort to reduce class size. Teachers have always universally supported this effort. Anyone who has ever been a classroom teacher knows that it is preferable to teach a group of fifteen students as opposed to one of thirty-five students. Perhaps the single most significant study on the importance of classroom size dealt with grades K–3. In the Star Study in Tennessee, a large group of students from varied communities were placed in control groups during their first four years of school. The study followed these students through their later school careers. Those students who were in small classes had and maintained higher test scores and experienced a smaller dropout rate. There was also a "decrease in the achievement gap between black and white students" who were in the smaller classes.[9] The Student Achievement Guarantee in Education (SAGE) study in Wisconsin verified the results in Tennessee. On the other hand, a project conducted by the Heritage Foundation "found that smaller class size did not boost achievement on the NAEP reading test."[10]

Reducing class size itself, especially at the secondary level, does not automatically result in increased student achievement. For the high school history teacher who lectures every class, whether it is fifteen or forty students, class size will probably not matter much. To make a difference, teachers must take advantage of smaller numbers to offer additional individual attention. They also must have the necessary space, equipment, and supplies. Most important, schools decreasing class size must ensure that the teachers they hire are well-trained and competent professionals. If done correctly, smaller classes are one way a principal can seek to increase student learning. The National Association of Elementary School Principals released the following position statement. "NAESP advocates that local school districts should develop a plan to facilitate the implementation of the recommended class-size ration of 15:1. . . . NAESP recognizes that class size is not the only determining factor, with research showing that more learning takes place when classes are small and teaching strategies are varied."[11]

The use of educational technology has also been hailed as a way to increase student learning. During the past fifteen years, school districts have spent billions of dollars to introduce computers into schools. Unfortunately, the money available for this initiative has been less than equal, with wealthy school districts quickly gaining Internet access, computer labs, and classroom computers, while poorer districts lag behind. Because of strong community support, it has been fairly easy for administrators to convince their school boards and the voters of their community of the need for educational computer hardware and software.

Principals have been expected to find ways to utilize this newest educational resource. Consultants were hired and schools began to include technology coordinators and technicians on their staff. Computer use in homes was increasing during the same period. In 1984, 8.2 percent of the homes in the United States had computers. By the year 2000, the percentage had increased to 51 percent, with 41.5 percent having Internet access. Among families with incomes of $75,000 or more, 88 percent had at least one computer. On the other hand, only 30 percent of single-parent homes had a computer in the year 2000. As parents experienced the importance of computers in their workplace, they became increasingly convinced that schools must prepare students for the technological world they would face. Whether or not this huge investment in technology has helped to increase student learning remains a highly debatable question.[12]

The *Harvard Education Letter* devoted an entire issue to this question. In an article entitled "Technology Works Best When It Serves Clear Education Goals," Donna Harrington-Lueker argues that training teachers is the key to the success of any technology program. She outlines five stages that teachers move through as they adopt the use of computers in their classroom. These steps include the following:

1. An entry stage, in which teachers struggled to master the nuts and bolts of using computers;
2. An adoption stage, in which teachers began using computer-based activities daily, but primarily for drill and practice;
3. An adaptation stage, in which teachers typically used computers as a way to increase student productivity (students could write better and faster using a word processor than they could by hand, for example);
4. An appropriation stage, in which teachers abandoned their effort to simply computerize traditional practices; and
5. An invention stage, where teacher began experimenting with new instructional patterns, such as interdisciplinary and project-based instruction or team teaching.[13]

Along with teacher training, it is necessary that a district develop a long-range technology plan. This plan should include measurable goals, a schedule for teacher and staff training, and an approach to maintaining and updating the equipment and software. Such a plan can be developed with the help of knowledgeable and skilled members of the community. Almost every district has citizens who have excellent backgrounds in the use of technology.

Even when all of these steps are taken, it is still questionable whether our large investment in technology has resulted in significant achievement gains in our schools. There are a number of major obstacles to the integration of technology in an educational setting. One of the big problems is providing the time to do what is necessary to make computers an effective tool in the classroom.

> Tony Pallija, principal at Max Hayes Vocational High School in Cleveland, Ohio, says time is one of the biggest obstacles. "Most in-service training after school is wasted on a tired staff. . . . We try to get grants to pay for substitutes to cover classes while teachers train in comfort and quiet."
>
> Lolli Haws agreed that time can be an obstacle. "The biggest obstacle for us is the time it takes for teachers to learn the technology skills, the time it takes to fully integrate technology into the curriculum the way it could be, and the time to share what we are doing so we can learn and get new ideas from each other."[14]

Despite widespread support for technology in schools, gaining enough money in the annual budget to maintain and update the system is frequently a problem. It is also difficult to find and keep top-notch technical support staff. These individuals can usually receive higher salaries working in industry. Without the necessary technical support, equipment breaks down and teachers become frustrated and discouraged. Finally, perhaps the biggest obstacle in introducing technology into the classroom is the reluctance of many teachers to change their ways. With all of these potential problems, the principal must be a catalyst and a supporter of technology if it is going to make a difference in schools.

Because it is quite certain that the use of computers will grow in importance in the twenty-first century, building administrators need to become knowledgeable and involved in their school's computer program. Younger teachers will increasingly bring to their classrooms additional knowledge and sophistication in the use of technology, and principals must be prepared to communicate with them and to encourage their efforts.

Whether it is through the use of technology or other innovative teaching techniques, schools will be called upon to integrate into their classrooms more special education students who had previously been in self-contained rooms with other students sharing a similar disability. Following the passage of federal Public Law 94-142, many districts identified their students with special educational needs and placed them in separate classrooms with certified special education teachers. Because of parental, judicial, and legislative pressures, more and more of these students are being brought back into regular classrooms. Special education teachers and aides have been assigned to help the classroom teacher in working with these children. Once again, it is the role of the principal to ensure that this change is successful. Providing faculty and staff with appropriate training is essential to the success of inclusion. Because there now are teams of people working in a classroom, time must be set aside for cooperative planning. Inclusion will not work if principals and other district administrators use it as a way to reduce the number of special education teachers and place too many special needs students in a single classroom.

Like the faculty and staff, building administrators too must learn to interact with students who are visually or hearing impaired, or physically or emotionally handicapped. The latter group can be a special problem for principals as they attempt to maintain student discipline in their building. Everyone in a school must become a special educator. Whatever an administrator's views may be concerning inclusion, a principal must continually articulate the advantages of the initiative, while at the same time realizing the challenges and potential problems it can cause. Thomas Reed and J. W. Good, after studying the "Attitudes of Rural School Principals toward Inclusive Practices and Placements for Students with Severe Disabilities," concluded that:

> The best principals enjoy and value every student for whom they bear responsibility and they continually seek appropriate programs for their schools. A rapidly growing "track record" indicates that inclusion will continue to be a viable strategy for educating students with severe disabilities. It is important for principals to be prepared and equipped to recommend all services within the special education continuum. As experience with students with severe disabilities increases, principals will be more likely to support, and even lead, restructuring efforts that favor inclusion. [15]

Like the idea of inclusion, the concept of school choice has become a major educational issue in the United States. During the 1950s, economist Milton Friedman suggested that creating competition between schools was the best way to bring about increased student learning. Because free public schools have had such an economic advantage over private schools, only those who can afford the additional cost of tuition have an equal opportunity to attend nonpublic schools. Even within a public school district, students have traditionally been assigned to the neighborhood school. The idea of choice—including the possibility of attending private religious schools—has been strongly supported in recent years by the Republican Party. Democrats have been less enthusiastic, especially since the two national teachers unions have not embraced the idea. Even with this formidable opposition, the movement toward choice and competition has gained support. Individual school districts have developed ways to give parents some opportunities in selecting a public school within the district. One of the first initiatives occurred primarily at the high school level in a number of urban districts. The practice of establishing magnet schools saw districts creating individual secondary programs with a specific focus that might appeal to students interested in that area. A city district might create a special school for those who are talented and interested in the arts. Admission to such a high school might well require students to have a music audition or present a portfolio of their artwork. Although such a school would have outstanding elective opportunities in art, music, and perhaps dance, they would still be required to meet all state and local district requirements.

Magnet schools remain directly under the jurisdiction of the central administration and of the board of education. The focus of other magnet schools might be in science, vocational education, or perhaps be an honors high school for outstanding students. Although the concept has spread in many larger cities, it is not really possible in smaller districts. Even where they have been established, there are still often neighborhood comprehensive high schools available for those students who are either unable or uninterested in attending a magnet school. A potential weakness of the system is that the student bodies of the comprehensive schools (high schools that provide a variety of majors) will lose many of their most talented students and perhaps become a "dumping ground" or a school of last resort.

Along with the idea of magnet schools, some districts are experimenting with a system of open enrollment. Instead of assigning students geographically to a certain building, families are allowed to apply to attend any elementary or secondary public school in the district. Open enrollment can promote limited competition within a district, but it can also create problems. For instance, the issue of transportation must be faced. If a plan assigns the transportation function to parents, many families will be unable to take advantage of the choices offered to them. As a result, critics would suggest that the system is undemocratic because parents who are affluent enough to transport their own children will have an unfair advantage. On the other hand, if the district accepts the responsibility of transporting students to the school of their choice, the resulting cost can be a burden to the taxpayers. In any case, open enrollment plans still only encompass the public schools located in a single district.

A more controversial but currently popular alternative is the creation of charter schools. In 1991, Minnesota's legislature authorized the establishment of charter schools. In just ten years, there were more than 2,000 such schools located in more than half of the states. Although the laws governing charter schools vary from state to state, all of the plans allow an individual or a group to apply to establish a charter school. Groups of teachers or a community organization frequently choose to come together to create a school plan with a specific focus. More recently, for-profit companies, which have been called Educational Maintenance Organizations, have become active in establishing charter schools. Companies such as the Edison Project and Tesseract (formerly Educational Alternatives Incorporated) are two prominent examples. A charter school usually has the following characteristics:

- Allows for the creation of a new or the conversion of an existing public school
- Prohibits admission tests
- Is nonsectarian
- Requires a demonstrable improvement in performance
- Can be closed if it does not meet expectations
- Does not need to conform to most state rules and regulations
- Receives funding based on the number of students enrolled[16]

The most politically charged of the plans to provide choice is the so-called voucher system. While public school professionals have accepted other choice plans, most have been strongly opposed to school vouchers. Plans differ, but in all the formulations, a government would provide to parents a voucher that families could use at any school to pay for their child's education. The most highly debated aspect of the plans is that in most cases the vouchers can be used to finance attendance at both public and private schools. Religious-based schools would be eligible to receive vouchers. Parents currently paying tuition to attend these schools would be beneficiaries of such a plan. Supporters argue that many poorer families who would like their children to be educated in a private school would be able to afford this option. Critics say that no voucher plan could possibly pay the tuition cost at our more exclusive private schools and that poorer students would still be excluded. For those opposing the plan, vouchers would merely subsidize more affluent parents who can already afford a private school education for their children. Others complain that the competition created by vouchers would only result in all schools spending large amounts of money to advertise and to recruit. These expenditures, they suggest, would be better used in an effort to improve our public schools.

Perhaps the most controversial aspect of the voucher plans is that it would allow public money to be used to directly subsidize religious education. This, in many people's eyes, would be a violation of the First Amendment of the U.S. Constitution, which has been used by the courts historically to define the appropriate relationship between church and state.

The constitutional issue raised by vouchers will ultimately be determined by the Supreme Court. In the summer of 2002, the Court did rule that the voucher plan in Cleveland, Ohio, was constitutional. The decision resulted in a rapid response by the National Association of Elementary School Principals. The statement said in part that:

> Now more than ever, as this nation's diversity increases, it is imperative that we maintain the separation of church and state by reserving public education funds for public schools. . . . Opening the door for public funds to be used by religious schools shows great misunderstanding and lack of respect for our nation's essential government document, the Constitution of the United States. This decision is a severe blow to public education and its already inadequate funding. It is disrespectful to the American taxpayer.

The association [NAESP] has a long record of opposition to vouchers—or public funds being diverted to other than public education. "Not only do our 29,000 members oppose vouchers, but so do the American people. . . . For over a decade opinion polls have consistently shown that the general public does not believe that public funds should pay for education in religious, or other non-public schools. Evidently, unlike the Supreme Court, the majority of Americans learned the basics of the First Amendment, which prohibits government support of religion."[17]

While a majority of the people questioned in the Delta Kappa/Gallup Poll opposed permitting parents to choose private schools for their students to attend at public expense, the number favoring such a policy rose from 34 percent in 2001 to 46 percent in 2002.[18] Currently, it is impossible to point to conclusive research on whether choice has brought about higher academic achievement. A major study in 2001 by RAND concluded that "exhaustive analysis backs neither camp in contentious debate."[19]

In commenting on the choice initiative, the RAND study made the following observation:

Whether the programs are large or small, the analysts stress, the specifics of policy design can have major consequences in maximizing the benefits that flow from vouchers and charters and minimizing harms. Their conditional recommendations to policymakers include the following:

- To promote academic effectiveness: permit existing schools (public, private, and parochial) to participate in choice programs, enforce testing requirements for all students, provide parents and public with plenty of information, and don't skimp on resources.
- To benefit those who remain in conventional public schools: require that all participating schools practice open admissions to prevent elite schools from "cream skimming" the best students, and give regular public schools the autonomy they need to perform in a newly competitive educational market.
- To ensure that voucher and charter schools serve low-income and special-needs students: fund choice programs through direct grants rather than income-tax subsidies, require open admissions, provide generous funding, and target specific students.[20]

Individual principals will not be responsible for deciding on the choice initiatives undertaken in their states and local school districts, but they and their organizations must become active participants in what will undoubtedly be an ongoing debate.

Along with choice, another area of controversy that will involve school leaders in the twenty-first century is multiculturalism. It is certainly true that:

> America's schools are changing. Walk onto the majority of playgrounds in this country, and immediately you will notice a diverse student body. Students of European ancestry play alongside students from Asia, Africa, and Central America. It's no news that immigration has been a part of this country's history. But in the last 10 years the nation's schools have seen a dramatic increase in the number of minority students—a trend that is predicted to continue. . . .
>
> According to the U.S. Department of Education's 1999 Digest of Education Statistics, from 1986 to 1997 the percentage of enrollment of African American, Hispanic, Asian, Pacific Islander, and Native American students increased, while that of white students decreased.
>
> And backed by the Kids Count 1997 report, this trend will continue. According to the report, by 2005 the number of Hispanic students in America's schools will increase by 30 percent; Asian and Pacific Islanders by 39 percent; and Native Americans by 6 percent.[21]

Pioneered by James A. Banks and others, the goal of multicultural education is to help students to celebrate diversity in the world and in the United States. Banks describes several approaches that can be used to help students develop more positive feelings towards different groups in our society.

1. Multicultural education often begins with the *contributions approach*, in which the study of ethnic heroes (for example, Sacajawea, Rosa Parks, or Booker T. Washington) is included in the curriculum. At this superficial contributions level, one might also find "food and festivals" being featured or such holidays as Cinco de Mayo being described or celebrated.
2. In the *additive approach*, a unit or course is incorporated, often but not always during a "special" week or month. February has become the month to study African Americans, while March has been designated "Women's History Month." Although these dedicated weeks and months offer a respite from the typical curricular material, no substantial change is made to the curriculum as a whole.

3. In the *transformation approach*, the entire Eurocentric nature of the curriculum is changed. Students are taught to view events and issues from diverse ethnic and cultural perspectives. For instance, the westward expansion of European descendants, or as an invasion from the East, through the eyes of Native Americans.[22]

Critics of multicultural education, such as E.D. Hirsch in his book *Cultural Literacy*, argue that instead of highlighting our differences, we should be using a core curriculum for all children. Such a curriculum would emphasize a common approach to subjects such as social studies and English. For Hirsch, children in the United States should learn about American heroes and read the classic books, poems, and plays by the giants of American and European literature. Multiculturalists would claim that our traditional approach to history has featured primarily white males and the same would be true with the authors who were studied in English classes. The debate might be described as to whether our schools should subscribe to the "melting pot" approach that attempts to make our diverse population into American citizens with a common educational heritage. For those who favor multiculturalism, the analogy would be the "salad bowl" approach, which has as its goal allowing various groups in our society to learn about their own heritage as well as that of others.

For the principal, this debate becomes very real when students or faculty request to sponsor a Black History Month or when parents of music students demand that students be introduced to Hispanic or Asian music. The discussion can also surface during discussions of what books students should be required to read or whether elementary children should do a major unit of study on their family's ancestors.

A relevant issue in the discussion concerning diversity in school districts is the question of affirmative action. Frequently, minority groups in a community will seek to have their school hire additional minority faculty. Too often, the race of the teachers in urban schools is predominately white, while the student body is made up primarily of nonwhite children. Principals and other administrators will be urged to hire more minority teachers to act as role models for the nonwhite students. School districts will increasingly face the challenge of creating a more diverse faculty even though there may be too few qualified minority candidates from which to choose. Affirmative action will remain an issue that divides our country.

There are other issues that can and do divide school communities. Sex education, especially the question of birth control, can raise the divisive topic of legalized abortion. A number of schools have attempted to minimize the controversy by using an "abstinence only" curriculum. Although such an approach does have support:

> it is not the choice of most schools, according to a new national survey of public secondary school principals by the Kaiser Family Foundation. While the study found messages about abstinence included in almost all sex education, it showed that most junior and senior high schools today take a more comprehensive approach, also including information about contraception and safer sex, rather than promoting abstinence until marriage as the *only* option.[23]

In a survey done in 1999, 48 percent of the principals reported a recent public debate on the topic of sex education. The subjects included the following:

- What topics to teach in sex education (26 percent);
- How parents give permission for students to take sex education (26 percent);
- Whether or not to teach sex education at all (17 percent); and
- Whether sex education should be single-sex or co-ed (16 percent).[24]

When creating new curriculum or changing the existing course of study, it is helpful to gain community input. Including physicians, psychologists, and clergy in such discussions can save the school district future problems. Such a committee should also include a broad cross-section of parents.

Secondary principals will periodically face an ongoing debate on eligibility policies for students participating in extracurricular activities, especially athletics. With the pressure to improve test scores, there will be additional motivation for schools to raise academic requirements for participation in clubs and sports teams. Critics of using grades as a "hammer" over students' heads see eligibility policies as being a source of discouragement for marginal students and perhaps for some a reason to drop out of school. Others point to the fact that these rules do cause student athletes to do their schoolwork. Where such policies exist, it is often the responsibility of the principal to see that they are enforced fairly.

Sometimes coaches and parents will attempt to influence the principal in carrying out the policy. To avoid too many problems, building administrators might follow the following guidelines:

1. Policies should be carefully worded to reduce the number of questions that can arise during enforcement. It would not be a bad idea to have the school attorney examine any proposed policy.
2. A single teacher probably should not have absolute power to make a student ineligible. The policy could require two unsatisfactory marks or be based on an overall grade percentage.
3. If possible, students in danger of becoming ineligible should be given a formal warning and sufficient time to raise their grades.
4. The period of eligibility should be short enough that students have the possibility of raising their grades and again becoming eligible. If students are made ineligible for the rest of the year or even an entire quarter, they will have less motivation to work hard to improve their grades.

Most important, it is absolutely necessary that the policy be consistently and fairly administrated. Any feeling that an administrator is showing favoritism or bowing to pressure could greatly harm the principal's reputation in the district.

Another concern common to many school administrators is the amount of paperwork that is now required in the position. For an article written jointly by the executive director of the Elementary and Secondary Principals Association, the authors asked practicing principals for examples of the paperwork dilemma that schools face.

From Kansas, came 31 pages of referral forms; then 59 pages of an Individualized Education Plan (IEP), which is required for every special education child. In these pages were six pages on procedures for tracheal suctioning with diagrams of the machine, saline solution, resuscitation bag, etc., which included two pages of possible problems that might require immediate attention, one page of problems that don't require immediate attention, and one page on how to clean the equipment and change the filter.

A Missouri principal took the state's motto to heart and showed us. She sent photos of paperwork next to a yardstick: three inches for a second grader; five inches for a third grader; and an overflowing file cabinet. A West Virginia member gave us a list of 20 steps in the paperwork process. These included team reports, forms that had to be filled out before and after a lot of procedures including testing; permissions sheets for parents; 14 pages for the IEP; and four different forms for Medicaid billing.

Furthermore, this principal pointed out that the IEP must be rewritten every year. And all of these forms are only part of it. Teachers must fill out normal lesson plans and progress reports. Program development by staff must also be done for each child on a daily basis to assure that the services are relevant and effective. This principal called the paperwork "the tail that wags the dog."[25]

The No Child Left Behind Act passed by Congress in 1991 has created the newest list of federal mandates. The National Association of Secondary School Principals described the act as "well-intentioned" but "causing confusion and worry."[26] The article goes on to say that:

The law is so complicated that a small industry is popping up to work on it. Law firms are specializing in it. Large school districts are adding employees to coordinate NCLB compliance. PR firms are approaching states with offers to help write report cards and craft language that parents can easily understand. Testing companies are getting ready to do a lot more business. Textbook companies are gearing up to sell reading books that pass the "scientifically based research" requirement. Websites are describing and defining the law and offering online training for educators. Workshops, seminars, and professional development programs are trying to address many aspects of NCLB.[27]

The growing amount of paperwork is one of the two major reasons that principals frequently feel overworked. "Seventy percent of the respondents said a lack of time was the biggest hurdle in their work, while 69 percent mentioned too much paperwork. Other hurdles included financial resources (51 percent), quality of teachers (34 percent), and burnout (28.5 percent)."[28]

All of these issues are raised not for the purpose of discouraging anyone from becoming a principal, but rather to give the reader a flavor of the varied challenges that the position offers. Managers in any field will face similar issues, and the successful principal will find ways to deal with them, along with the multitude of dilemmas, which are all but inevitable. One of the concerns that will undoubtedly involve building administrators will be the area of school law. This complex but very real aspect of a principal's work deserves its own separate chapter.

NOTES

1. Richard W. Stevenson, "Amid Criticism, Bush Promises to Produce Education Gains," *New York Times*, 9 January 2003, at www.nytimes.com/2003/01/09/politics/09BUSH.html?pagewanted=print&position=t… (accessed 14 January 2003).

2. National Association of Secondary School Principals, "High Stakes' Testing," *National Association of Secondary School Principals*, 8 March 2001, at www.nassp.org/publicaffairs/ps_hi_stks_tstng.htm (accessed 1 February 2003).

3. National Association of Secondary School Principals, "High Stakes' Testing."

4. W. James Popham, "The Mismeasurement of Educational Quality," *American Association of School Administrators*, December 2000, at www.aasa.org/publications/sa/2000_12/popham_mismeasurement.htm (accessed 21 February 2003).

5. Popham, "The Mismeasurement of Educational Quality."

6. Marlow Ediger, "The School Principal: State Standards versus Creativity," *Journal of Instructional Psychology* 28, no. 2 (June 2001): 79–83.

7. National Association of Elementary School Principals, "High-Stakes Cheating," *National Association of Elementary School Principals: Communicator*, February 2000, at www.naesp.org/comm/c0200.htm (accessed 1 February 2003).

8. Poster published by Midstate School Finance Consortium; source for all data: New York State Department of Education 2000–2001.

9. National Association of Elementary School Principals, "Does Size Really Matter?" *National Association of Elementary School Principals: Communicator*, December 2000, at www.naesp.org/comm/c1200.htm (accessed 1 February 2003).

10. National Association of Elementary School Principals, "Does Size Really Matter?"

11. National Association of Elementary School Principals, "Does Size Really Matter?"

12. U.S. Census Bureau, "Home Computers and Internet Use in the United States," *U.S. Census Bureau: Special Studies* (September 2001).

13. Donna Harrington-Lueker, "Technology Works Best When It Serves Clear Educational Goals," *Harvard Education Letter* 8, no. 6 (November/ December 1997).

14. Gary Hopkins, "Principals Talk Tech: How Is Technology Integration Going?" *Education World*, 30 April 2002, at www.education-world.com/a_ admin/admin268.shtml (accessed 1 February 2003).

15. Martha Livingston, Thomas Reed, and J. W. Good, "Attitudes of Rural School Principals toward Inclusive Practices and Placements for Students with Severe Disabilities," *Journal of Research for Educational Leaders* (Fall 2001).

16. Myra Pollack Sadker and David Miller Sadker, *Teachers, Schools, and Society*, 5th ed. (Boston: McGraw-Hill, 2000), 156.

17. National Association of Elementary School Principals, "Principals Discouraged by Supreme Court's School Voucher Decision," *National Association of Elementary School Principals News*, 27 June 2002, at www.naesp.org/comm/ prss6-27-02.htm (accessed 21 February 2003).

18. Phi Delta Kappa International, "School Improvement in the Spotlight," *2002 Poll Press Release*, 20 August 2002, at www.pdkintl.org/adv/02pollpr.htm (accessed 1 February 2003).

19. Jess Cook, "RAND Study Examines the Evidence on Vouchers and Charter Schools," *RAND News Release*, 6 December 2001, at www.rand.org/ hot/Press/vouchers.html (accessed 1 February 2003).

20. Cook, "RAND Study Examines the Evidence on Vouchers and Charter Schools."

21. National Association of Elementary School Principals, "The Changing Face of Education," *Communicator*, March 2000, at www.naesp.org/comm/ c0300.htm (accessed 21 February 2003).

22. Sadker and Sadker, *Teachers, Schools, and Society*, 54–55.

23. Amy Weitz, "Most Secondary Schools Take a More Comprehensive Approach to Sex Education," *The Henry J. Kaiser Family Foundation News Release*, 14 December 1999, at www.kff.org/content/1999/1560/PressRelease-sexed.htm (accessed 1 February 2003).

24. Weitz, "Most Secondary Schools Take a More Comprehensive Approach to Sex Education."

25. Gerald N. Tirozzi and Vincent L. Ferrandino, "Prisoners of Paperwork," *National Association of Secondary School Principals*, 2002, at www.nassp.org/ publicaffairs/views/paperwork.htm (accessed 1 February 2003).

26. Gerald N. Tirozzi and Vincent L. Ferrandino, "Getting Ahead of No Child Left Behind," *National Association of Secondary School Principals*, 2002, at www.nassp.org/publicaffairs/views/get_ahead_nclb.htm (accessed 1 February 2003).

27. Tirozzi and Ferrandino, "Getting Ahead of No Child Left Behind."

28. Mark Stricherz, "School Leaders Feel Overworked, Survey Finds," *Education Week*, 21 November 2001, at www.edweek/org/ew/ew_printstory .cfm?slug=12agenda.h21 (accessed 13 January 2003).

(12)

THE PRINCIPAL AND THE LAW

Principals do not have to be lawyers but they must remain informed in the area of school law. Most administrative certification programs will require at least one course in the subject, but this will only provide a starting point for school administrators. Since the law is always in flux, national and state administrative organizations will offer a significant amount of information in their publications concerning laws and court cases. One of the most confusing aspects of school law is that there are many sources of law that can affect a principal.

At the federal level, legislation passed by Congress increasingly has a major impact on schools. For most of our nation's history, the primary source of school law originated at the state level; however, the federal government has become progressively more active in the field of education. Perhaps the two most significant federal laws are PL 94-142 (1975) and the more recent No Child Left Behind Act (2001). Public Law 94-142 and its subsequent amendments established the regulations for identifying and providing appropriate educational services for students identified as needing special education. Nationwide, approximately 11 percent of the public school students have been designated as being in need of special education services. The placements range from special residential schools to services in an inclusion classroom.

Principals are responsible for helping to administer referrals to the Committee on Special Education and, following the student's classification by the committee, ensuring that the Individualized Educational Plan of each student is properly carried out. Even though the principals might not be actively involved in the day-to-day details of administering special education law, there is no question that building administrators will be held responsible if violations of the law or regulations occur in their school. The No Child Left Behind Act also is currently engaging principals in a learning process to ensure proper implementation in their districts and their specific building.

The decisions of the federal courts also have a major impact on schools. Perhaps the single most significant case was *Brown vs. Topeka, Kansas* (1954). This landmark decision ruled unconstitutional the "separate but equal doctrine" that permitted separate schools for black and white students. In an attempt to integrate our schools, the nation went through a period of bussing programs and introduced the idea of affirmative action. Additional cases have defined the limits of the federal government in attempting to integrate our schools.

State courts also frequently deal with cases affecting schools. Most recently, there have been challenges to the validity of state financial aid programs in providing equality of opportunity to the students of the state. A number of decisions have ruled that the current methods used by a state for funding schools are not acceptable. These decisions have mandated that the state legislature must create funding formulas that are more helpful to districts with low property values. State courts have also dealt with legal complaints concerning special education services. It is important that principals remain current with the case law that evolves from both the state and federal courts, especially in areas such as the church and state controversy.

Along with court decisions, the chief executive or agencies of the state education department have the power to make decisions that have the force of law in some states. For instance, the commissioner of education in New York State hears cases on controversial issues submitted by residents of the state, and the written decisions of the commissioner have the force of law in New York State. Finally, it is the state legislatures whose statutes most regularly affect schools. Since the adoption of the Constitution, education has been considered a "reserved power" of the states. In most states, there is also some sort of statewide board of education that operates along with the state legislature and the governor in developing and enforcing school law and policy.

With all of these varied sources of law and policy, school administrators are bound to be affected. There will be occasions when principals are confronted with situations that will require advice from an attorney. Even when principals are fairly certain that they understand the law, it is best to seek a legal opinion if there is any question.

State administrative and school board associations often have legal staff or attorneys on retainer who are specialists in school law. Contacting these individuals is always a possibility and because dues are paid to the organization, the calls are usually free to members. The services of these organizations are not likely to include legal representation in a school-related lawsuit, unless it happens to be a case that could have major implications for the membership of the organization. Still, the organization attorneys can give information over the phone, which can give administrators the resources they need when reacting to a problem.

The school attorney will most often provide legal advice to the administration and the board of education. In any potential legal situation, it is wise for the principals to discuss the matter with their superintendent or their direct superior in the organization. Despite the fact that most school administrators like to solve their own problems, it is important that building-level principals do not put their district in a position where a law or a state policy is being violated. At the same time, unless the attorney is on the district payroll or on a retainer, principals must remember that lawyers charge by the minute. Telephone calls to an attorney are not the time to talk about the family or one's golf scores. Although it is certain that principals will continue to have occasions to work with lawyers, it is difficult to predict the specific areas that might result in litigation in any district. Using the past as a guide, there are certainly several issues that have created legal problems for schools.

The question of the appropriate relationship of church and state has been mentioned in regard to the issue of school choice, but there are a number of other potential concerns involving religion that can arise for a building administrator. In an attempt to foresee potential problems in this sensitive area, it is wise if principals have a deep knowledge of their community. There are districts that have active, conservative Christian groups, while other communities may have significant numbers of people of the Jewish, Muslim, or other faith. Understanding the religious groups that make up a community is not enough, as in any district one family or one person can challenge a district's actions in court. The only answer is to attempt to obey the law as the courts are currently construing it or be willing to take on a legal battle if the board of education feels that it is appropriate.

The difficulty facing schools in this area is highlighted in a recent article in the *Christian Science Monitor*, which includes this statement:

America's public schools are in a bind. A new law requires them to allow "religious expression" on school grounds—or risk losing federal funds. But they risk a lawsuit if they do. . . .

If schools allow any religious speech at a graduation ceremony, most are aware that they could face a lawsuit. But now, if they don't—according to the dictates of the NCLB [No Child Left Behind]—they could risk losing federal funds.[1]

Because of conflicting lower court decisions in different federal jurisdictions,

it remains unclear if it is legal for a student giving a graduation speech to use that speech as a platform for prayer. However, the Court has declared that student-led public prayers at athletic events constitute school sponsorship of religion, a violation of the establishment clause of the First Amendment. Finally the legality of observing a moment of silence in schools varies by state, and educators are encouraged to check their school policies.[2]

In a related issue, schools can currently allow student religious groups to meet in a school building as long as other nonreligious groups are allowed to use the facilities and if school employees do not lead the group. Teachers and other staff can be present for a Bible study group, but not be the leaders of such an organization.

Although the Clinton administration published a list of helpful guidelines to assist school administrators in dealing with church and state issues, new guidelines prepared by the Bush administration have introduced some apparent changes.

One is the way they treat the question of "religious expression" at assemblies. While the Clinton guidelines stressed that "the right of religious expression in school does not include the right to have a 'captive audience' listen," the Bush guidelines draw a different conclusion.

They acknowledge that prayer or religious speech initiated by school officials would be illegal but then assert that "the speech of students who choose to express themselves through religious means such as prayer is not attributable to the state, and therefore may not be restricted because of its religious content."

But that advice is not consistent with some recent court rulings, say legal experts, and could be dangerous for school systems if they assume that by relying on the guidelines they'll be in accord with the law.[3]

As administrators attempt to understand the current status of the law, it is important to keep in mind the decision of the Supreme Court in the case *Santa Fe Independent School District vs. Doe*, which dealt with a student-led and initiated prayer at the high school football games. The Court ruled that such a prayer was in violation of the First Amendment.[4] This decision, like any of the cases in this area of the law, could be reversed in the future as more conservative judges are appointed to the federal bench. School administrators must understand that these cases depend on how judges interpret the meaning of the phrases in the First Amendment of the U.S. Constitution, which states that "Congress shall make no law respecting an establishment of religion, or prohibiting the free exercise thereof." [5] All that a principal can do with cases involving religion is to attempt to remain current; if a difficult question arises, seek legal counsel.

An equally dynamic and flexible issue is the question of student rights. Recently, the question of the right of schools to test students for drugs has arisen. In the Supreme Court case, the issue revolved around the Fourth Amendment of the U.S. Constitution, which prohibits "unreasonable" searches and seizures. A South Carolina decision in June 2002 allowed schools to establish "random, suspicionless urinalysis tests for students participating in extracurricular activities."[6] Although this decision gave to schools an additional weapon in fighting drug use, it cannot be inferred that all searches of students by school employees are legal. While using dogs to search lockers has been declared legal, using them to "sniff students (rather than things) is allowable only if the dogs are reliable and the student is a reasonable suspect. The strip search is illegal."[7]

Principals who choose to search a student's locker or car might be advised to take along a witness. It also might be prudent to have the student present. In recent years, courts have given school administrators additional leeway in conducting random searches, and the qualification that a principal must have "reasonable cause" to conduct a search has been weakened. Even though administrative prerogatives have been broadened, principals would be advised not to overdo the power to search student lockers.

Another student right that has been challenged in the courts relates to the question of the freedom of the student press. If a school newspaper is part of a journalism class or financially supported by the school district, administrators have the right to censor or curtail the publication. A paper that is not sponsored by the school has more latitude, but would be subject to administrative oversight if it included obscenity, did psychological harm, or could be proven to be disruptive.[8]

Student freedom of speech issues have also been raised as a result of clothing worn in school. The landmark case was *Tinker vs. Des Moines, SD* in 1969. In this case, students wore black armbands to protest the involvement of the United States in Vietnam. The court upheld the students' right to carry on this type of protest, as it was not considered disruptive. Students can wear badges or buttons as long as they are not obscene, liable, or advocate racial or religious prejudice.[9] At times, students will wear T-shirts that have slogans that might at least appear to advocate the use of drugs or alcohol. Although school officials must be careful, they can prohibit any clothing that might be "disruptive." A quiet, private conversation asking a student to change the shirt is often preferable to solving the problem using a suspension.

Student rights in regard to suspensions vary from state to state, and it is essential that principals totally understand the laws regulating this important administrative power. At the very least, students have the right to be personally informed of the reason for their suspension and the evidence of their guilt. Equally important is that students who are about to be suspended should have the right to explain themselves. Depending on state law, a building principal can be delegated the power to suspend for up to five to ten days. Beyond whatever the state limit is, students must be given formal due process. Most often this includes the right to be represented by an attorney, to call witnesses, and to question witnesses who are testifying against them. Such a hearing is usually held before the superintendent or a qualified hearing officer appointed by the superintendent. In smaller districts, the board of education might hear the case of a student being considered for a long-term suspension. It is not unusual that the building principal might act as the "prosecutor" in cases involving extended suspensions. This type of disciplinary action is rare and, when it is used, building principals must carefully prepare the case. Other less drastic forms of punishment should be considered before resorting to a lengthy suspension. When such action seems the most appropriate alternative, it would sometimes be wise to involve the school attorney. As schools seek to ensure a safe environment for all students through approaches such as zero tolerance, it remains important that principals do whatever is necessary to protect the legal rights of students.

As one considers disciplinary tools used by administrators, the issue of corporal punishment becomes paramount. Not too many years ago, principals frequently used a paddle to punish unruly students. Other forms of physical force were also prevalent in some schools. Although in 1977 the Supreme Court authorized states to allow corporal punishment that was reasonable and not excessive, many states and school districts have chosen to prohibit any physical punishment of students. Where it is allowed, there are very specific restrictions in district policies.[10] Whatever a state or district policy is concerning corporal punishment, principals should not rely on physical force to maintain discipline in their schools. On the other hand, when it is necessary to protect students or staff or in self-defense, a school administrator would be expected to use whatever force is necessary. Given the number of cases in the courts involving harassment, a school administrator should advise faculty and staff to refrain from using physical force, except in emergency situations.

Whatever the circumstances, administrators or faculty who touch students in any way could face legal charges. The issue of sexual harassment has become prominent in the United States, beginning with the hearings on the Supreme Court appointment of Clarence Thomas. Anita Hill's testimony to a Senate committee raised the issue to a nationwide concern.

Businesses and school districts have since been busy creating sexual harassment policies to help them deal with charges within their institutions. Any school without such a policy should quickly adopt one. Most district plans include the appointment of a "sexual harassment officer" who is available to students and employees alike. If this individual is unable to resolve any situation reported to them, the policy would call for additional steps to be taken by the district. Failure to deal appropriately with charges of sexual harassment can have a very negative impact on a school district because the Supreme Court has ruled that a victim of sexual harassment can receive monetary damages from a school district that has failed to act appropriately. Usually, a student or employee will first file a grievance with the office of civil rights, but it is not unusual for someone to also sue the school district.[11]

The courts have identified two types of sexual harassment. The first has been labeled *quid pro quo harassment*. This type of offense:

> occurs when a school employee causes a student to believe that he or she must submit to unwelcome sexual conduct in order to participate in a school program or activity. It can also occur when an employee causes a student to believe that the employee will make an educational decision based on whether or not the student submits to unwelcome sexual conduct. For example, when a teacher threatens to fail a student unless the student agrees to date the teacher, it is quid pro quo harassment.[12]

The second type of offense has been labeled *hostile environment harassment*, which:

> occurs when unwelcome sexually harassing conduct is so severe, persistent, or pervasive that it affects a student's ability to participate in or benefit from an education program or activity, or creates an intimidating, threatening, or abusive educational environment. A hostile environment can be created by a school employee, another student, or even someone visiting the school, such as a student or employee from another school.[13]

Because schools can be held financially liable for failing to act appropriately to complaints regarding sexual harassment, it is important that any policy be examined by a competent attorney. As the building principal, it is absolutely essential that every charge be carefully investigated under the terms of the policy. Any action that might be construed as a cover-up by a school official can lead to serious difficulty for the school district. Sexual harassment issues are not the only ones for which a school district or an administrator can be held legally responsible.

Despite the fact that all schools carry liability insurance on employees, principals should do everything possible to ensure that their schools do not become involved in negligence suits. One of the areas that principals must be extremely careful about is the need to provide adequate adult supervision at all times. An accident on a playground where 125 fourth graders are playing on slides, swings, and other apparatus, where one teacher is watching the entire area, while the other four teachers are drinking coffee in the faculty room, could easily lead to a lawsuit based on inadequate supervision. Any time a teacher leaves students unattended, there is the possibility of an accident that could lead to a lawsuit. Gym classes, science labs, and shops are all high-risk areas where adequate supervision is required.

Several other areas can create legal problems for administrators. High schools are frequently recipients of donations for awards and scholarships. Although such gifts are greatly appreciated, administrators must be careful that the selection process and the qualifications for the award are not discriminatory. Establishing a prize for the outstanding male athlete without a corresponding award for a female athlete could be judged a violation of Title IX of federal law.

Laws also govern student records:

> Parents must be allowed to inspect their children's student records. The federal Family Educational Rights and Privacy Act (FERPA), also known as the Buckley Amendment, denies federal funds to any school or college that fails to allow a student or his or her parents to inspect or challenge the student's records. Under the Buckley Amendment, parents also have the right to refuse to allow districts to disclose what is known as directory information (personally identifying information about students such as their names, addresses, Social Security numbers, for example) about their children that districts otherwise may choose to release under specified circumstances.
>
> However, it is advisable to have appropriate personnel present when parents are actually inspecting student records to help explain the records and prevent any misinterpretation by the parent.[14]

Once students reach their eighteenth birthday, they, too, have access to their own records and can grant permission for others to view their records. For a principal, it is important to have guidelines within the school as to what will be placed in a student's official records. Especially sensitive are notes written to the principal about students by faculty members, counselors, or psychologists. Other sensitive information includes certain health issues. This is especially true because faculty and other professional staff have access to student records. A particularly controversial issue is the record of a student who is HIV infected. "To date, however, HIV-infected students and teachers are not viewed as a significant risk to the health of the rest of the population and cannot be denied their educational rights."[15] In addition, it appears that information concerning a student with this condition should not be allowed to become public knowledge.

Along with potential legal problems related to students, principals must consider potential lawsuits involving faculty and staff. As part of the team involved in the hiring process, building administrators must be very careful not to engage in activities that could lead to charges of discrimination. When interviewing female candidates, one should not ask them questions about their plans for having children. Such a question might be interpreted as a way to seek information about potential maternity leaves that the candidate might seek in the future. Other potential areas of discrimination in hiring or dismissing employees would be discrimination on the basis of age, gender, race, religion, or disability. Except in eleven states and 160 cities and counties, discrimination on the basis of sexual preference is not forbidden.[16] In this regard, administrators should know the law in their own city or state when dealing with known homosexual applicants or employees. It is possible that in the future there will be legislation at the national level mandating a nondiscrimination policy for homosexuals.

The personal lifestyle of faculty and staff can also present problems for a principal. Some teachers and staff members might drink excessively or live with someone of the opposite sex to whom they are not married. Women teachers could become pregnant even though they are unmarried. The legal principle that school administrators should consider in dealing with an employee's personal life could currently be summarized as follows. Does the behavior "significantly disrupt the educational process"?[17] In determining this disruption, the school district must prove that the behavior erodes the employee's "credibility with students, colleagues, or the community."[18] Before an administrator seeks to discipline or dismiss a faculty or staff member for behavior outside of school, it is wise to seek the advice of the school attorney. If it is a controversial area of behavior, administrators should expect that employee unions would mount a spirited defense of their member.

Unions will also vigorously protect an employee's right to freedom of speech. Employees working for a school district have the legal right to publicly criticize their school district, as long as they are not purposely misrepresenting the facts. Administrators may well find themselves being criticized by a district employee in a public budget hearing or in a letter to the editor in the local paper. As a public figure, principals will occasionally be targets of community critics. In responding to letters to the local newspaper, there are times when a principal is wise to remain silent. A public response can lead to a series of letters that can keep a controversy alive for an extended period. The only legal restrictions on an employee's freedom of speech would be if the statement was "intentionally or recklessly inaccurate, disclosed confidential material, or hampered either school discipline" or the performance of an administrator's duties.[19]

Faculty rights can also be involved in legal questions related to the choice of educational materials and instructional methods. Teachers sometimes will resist administrative or board interference in the name of academic freedom. The courts have attempted to find a balance between teacher rights and the responsibility of the school district to ensure that students are exposed to appropriate subject matter in a setting that is conducive to effective teaching and learning. Judicial decisions have offered the following guidelines: Materials must be appropriate and relevant to the topics outlined in the course syllabus. In addition, they must not be obscene or "substantially disruptive of school discipline."[20]

Sometimes a more difficult judgment has to be made by a principal when students or parents complain about a teacher who wastes time in class talking about subjects that are unrelated to the curriculum. For instance, you might have an instructor who is also the wrestling coach spending time talking about wrestling in biology class. Other teachers tend to dwell on stories about themselves or their family. A quiet conversation with the teacher involved can usually modify such behavior, but there are times when administrative involvement in what is going on in a classroom can touch off a larger discussion relating to academic freedom. Teachers' unions are often very protective of a member's prerogatives in their own classroom.

With regard to the selection of materials either for classroom use or in the school library, every district should have in place a policy that creates a process for parents to appeal the use of any book, periodical, speaker, or any other learning material. The written policy should include the standards used by the school in selecting materials; librarians especially should be prepared to defend their selections using such sources as the recommended materials of the American Library Association. The magnitude of the problem can be seen by the fact that between 1990 and 1999 there were 5,718 challenges to library materials purchased by school districts. The most frequently challenged books in the year 2000 were as follows:

- *Harry Potter* series, J. K. Rowling
- *The Chocolate War*, Robert Cormier
- *Alice* series, Phyllis Reynolds Naylor
- *Killing Mr. Griffin*, Lois Duncan
- *Of Mice and Men*, John Steinbeck
- *I Know Why the Caged Bird Sings*, Maya Angelou
- *Fallen Angels*, Walter Dean Myers
- *Scary Stories* series, Alvin Schwartz
- *The Terrorist*, Caroline Cooney
- *The Giver*, Lois Lowry[21]

With a policy in place that carefully considers all purchases of materials and a defensible appeals process, principals can rely on other professionals to avoid divisive conflicts and inappropriate censorship in their school. Equal caution must be exercised in the selection of plays that will be publicly performed. A school production of *Inherit the Wind*, a dramatization of the Scopes trial, can anger conservative Christians and create a major controversy in some communities. Such a problem might occur because for some viewers the play appears to make light of a literal interpretation of the Bible.

In some school districts, a student concert in December that includes Christmas carols can be found to be inappropriate by some non-Christians. Many districts have changed the name of the performance from the Christmas concert to the Holiday or Winter concert. Christmas or Easter decorations, especially in the classroom, can also bring objections from some parents. With all of these issues, there is some guidance in current case law, but the district must weigh whether it wishes to spend taxpayer money on the legal cost of defending the right to have Christmas trees in the classroom. Occasionally, boards of education feel strongly enough about such an issue that they are willing to be a test case. Obviously when making such a decision, it is important that the district have a good chance of winning in court and also have the majority of the community supporting such a lawsuit. When there is the potential for a legal challenge, principals are wise to consult with their superintendent.

A more recent legal dilemma for schools is the issue of the use of the Internet in schools. Congress has passed laws that make a serious effort to protect children from inappropriate Internet sites. Some of this legislation has been challenged as being in violation of the First Amendment, but it appears that currently courts are giving schools and parents significant power in controlling Internet use by minors. In fact, the Children's Internet Protection Act, passed in 2000, mandates that schools receiving federal funds have in place policies that protect children from inappropriate Internet sites. It remains true, however, that current laws do not provide complete protection. The National Association of Secondary School Principals has concluded in a public statement that:

> schools and parents alike must educate students on how to effectively and appropriately use the wealth of resources available on the World Wide Web. Congress has made significant and profound efforts to offer legislation that will protect children. These statutes, in combination with efforts of parents, teachers, and school administrators, should enable students to safely and appropriately further themselves personally and educationally with the information and resources that the Internet provides.[22]

One final very unpleasant legal issue too often involves building principals. During the past twenty years, almost three million cases of child abuse have been reported in the United States.[23] Child abuse and neglect can include any of the following:

- Physical abuse, evidenced by cuts, welts, burns, and bruises
- Sexual molestation and exploitation
- Neglect: medical, educational, or physical
- Emotional abuse[24]

Local child protection agencies are available to school administrators when they become aware of a possible incident of child abuse or neglect. These agencies will quickly investigate any report and sometimes remove a child from an unsafe home environment. Many schools have a policy that requires that faculty and staff to immediately report possible abuse cases to the building principal. It then becomes the school administrator's job to telephone the appropriate agency. Usually such calls remain anonymous, although there are times when a principal will be drawn directly into a case. In many jurisdictions, school personnel are "mandated reporters," who under the law have no option but to report suspected abuse. Principals are wise not to try to deal with such reports by themselves. Agencies with trained professionals are better equipped to investigate such cases.

Although building administrators are not too often called into court in child abuse cases, it is possible that in family custody disputes that school personnel will be called as witnesses to testify on a child's behavior and progress in school. With parents who are disputing custody, there is also the potential problem that a parent from a broken marriage who does not have legal rights will try to sign a son or daughter out of school. In extreme cases, children have been kidnapped from school by a desperate parent who has been denied parental rights by the courts. For that reason, it is essential that school records include information on parents with and without legal custody and that school office personnel are trained to notify the principal immediately of any possible violation of a court order dealing with custody. The fact is that schools must be very careful in releasing students to anyone who does not have legal custody or who has not gained prior approval from a parent or guardian.

When one considers the many issues discussed in the past two chapters, the reader could easily conclude that it is much easier to remain a classroom teacher and forget the idea of administration. The truth is that a principal with an adequate knowledge of the law and well-thought-out administrative policies can most often avoid becoming involved in litigation. The ability to work effectively in this area is important, but not the only factor that will ensure a principal's success. A good deal of research in recent years has attempted to pinpoint the characteristics of a successful principal. Careful consideration of this research should be helpful to anyone considering a career in school administration.

NOTES

1. Marjorie Coeyman, "Religion-free Zone?" *The Christian Science Monitor*, 20 May 2003, at www.csmonitor.com/2003/0520/p11s01-lepr.htm (accessed 5 June 2003).

2. Myra Pollack Sadker and David Miller Sadker, *Teachers, Schools, and Society* (Boston: McGraw-Hill, 2003), 440.

3. Coeyman, "Religion-free Zone?"

4. David C. Bloomfield, "The Doomsday Walls of Church-State Separation," *American Association of School* Administrators, February 2001, at www.aasa.org/publications/sa/2001_02/colbloomfield.htm (accessed 21 Feb. 2003).

5. Bernard A. Weisberger, *The Impact of Our Past: A History of the United States* (New York: American Heritage, 1972), 788.

6. National Association of Secondary School Principals, "Supreme Court Broadens Scope of Drug Testing in Schools," *National Association of Secondary School Principals*, at www.nassp.org/services/legal_drugtstng.html (accessed 1 February 2003).

7. Sadker and Sadker, *Teachers, Schools, and Society*, 441.

8. Sadker and Sadker, *Teachers, Schools, and Society*, 443.

9. New York State School Boards Association, *School Law*, 25th ed. (Albany: New York State School Boards Association, 1994), 250.

10. Sadker and Sadker, *Teachers, Schools, and Society*, 438.

11. Sadker and Sadker, *Teachers, Schools, and Society*, 426–27.

12. Office for Civil Rights, "Sexual Harassment: It's Not Academic," *ED/Office for Civil Rights*, 28 December 2000, at www.ed.gov/offices/OCR/docs/ocrshpam.html (accessed 20 February 2003).

13. Office for Civil Rights, "Sexual Harassment: It's Not Academic."

14. New York State School Boards Association, *School Law*, 40–41.

15. Louis Fischer, David Schimmel, and Cynthia Kelly, *Teachers and the Law* (New York: Longman, 1999), as printed in Sadker and Sadker, *Teachers, Schools, and Society*, 443.

16. Sadker and Sadker, *Teachers, Schools, and Society*, 427.

17. Sadker and Sadker, *Teachers, Schools, and Society*, 427.

18. Sadker and Sadker, *Teachers, Schools, and Society*, 427.

19. Sadker and Sadker, *Teachers, Schools, and Society*, 430.

20. Sadker and Sadker, *Teachers, Schools, and Society*, 428–29.

21. "Ten Most Challenged Books in 2000," Office for Intellectual Freedom, American Library Association on the Web, 2001, as printed in Sadker and Sadker, *Teachers, Schools, and Society*, 283.

22. National Association of Secondary School Principals, "Protecting Children on the Internet," *National Association of Secondary School Principals*, at www.nassp.org/services/legal_chldnet.html (accessed 1 February 2003).

23. Fred Hechinger, *Fateful Choices: Healthy Youth for the Twenty-first Century* (New York: Carnegie Council on Adolescent Development, 1992); Administration for Children and Families U.S. Department of Health and Human Services, ACF Press Room: HHS News, *HHS Reports New Child Abuse and Neglect Statistics* (Washington, D.C.: April 2, 2001), as printed in Sadker and Sadker, *Teachers, Schools, and Society*, 447.

24. Jan English and Anthony Papalia, "The Responsibility of Educators in Cases of Child Abuse and Neglect," *Chronicle Guidance* (January 1988), 88–89; Carol K. Sigelman and David R. Shaffer, *Life-Span Human Development*, 3rd ed. (Pacific Grove, Calif.: Wadsworth Publishing, 1999), as printed in Sadker and Sadker, *Teachers, Schools, and Society*, 447.

⓭

SUCCEEDING AS A PRINCIPAL

Numerous studies and individual authors have attemted to identify the traits, skills, and attitudes that are common in those individuals who are effective in the role of the building principal. Everything that has been written on the subject has concluded that the position is indeed a challenging one. Rick DuFour states the difficulties as follows:

> Principals have been called upon to:
> - Celebrate the success of their schools and to perpetuate discontent with the status quo;
> - Convey urgency regarding the need for school improvement and to demonstrate the patience that sustains improvement efforts over the long haul;
> - Encourage individual autonomy and to insist on adherence to the school's mission, vision, values, and goals;
> - Build widespread support for change and to push forward with improvement despite resisters;
> - Approach improvement incrementally and to promote the aggressive, comprehensive shakeup necessary to escape the bonds of traditional school cultures.[1]

Despite these seemingly contradictory expectations, researchers agree that principals are a key factor in the success of any school. Bess Keller, in an article published in *Education Week,* writes that:

> If there is one broad area of agreement among researchers, consultants, those who teach prospective principals, and the principals themselves, it is that schools must have a clear idea of what they are about.
>
> Leaders "must understand the mission of the school, promote it, use an educational agenda, and keep it in front of people."[2]

It is the principal's job to articulate the mission of the school in a way that faculty, staff, students, and parents understand the goals of the district. The administrator then must find ways to work with all of these stakeholders to make the vision a reality. Currently, the type of vision that is spoken of most often includes the idea of creating a learning community in which everyone involved with the school is engaged in learning. This must take place in an environment in which every person is treated with respect and dignity.

Although a vision is a necessary first step, it is not enough to ensure the success of a principal or a school. Adolf Hitler had a vision, as did Joseph Stalin. Visions must be appropriate and obtainable. It is also true that without positive values, any plan can easily result in negative outcomes. Administrators must seek their objectives in a way that demonstrates a clear understanding of right and wrong. Some principals work under the Machiavellian principle that the "ends justify the means." Such administrators can justify lying, or at least bending the truth; they can also destroy the careers of those who oppose them. Other building leaders are respected for not lying or taking advantage of others. These individuals have earned the reputation of being honest, fair, and truly caring about other people. In an article entitled "Lead with Soul and Spirit," Lee G. Bolman and Terrence E. Deal suggest that "effective leadership in challenging times boils down to qualities such as focus, passion, and integrity."[3] Warren Buffett lists first the quality of integrity in his characteristics essential in a leader.[4] There is, in the words of Michael Fullan, an "expanding interest in moral and spiritual leadership in education."[5]

Whether one chooses to think in terms of spiritual leadership, soul, or values, there is no question that a successful principal must be an honest and ethical individual. To highlight the importance of this essential characteristic, the National Association of Elementary School Principals has developed for its members a Statement of Ethics for School Administrators. The ethical standards identified are:

1. Makes the well-being of students the fundamental value in all decision making and actions.
2. Fulfills professional responsibilities with honesty and integrity.
3. Supports the principle of due process and protects the civil and human rights of all individuals.
4. Obeys local, state, and national laws.
5. Implements the governing board of education's policies and administrative rules and regulations.
6. Pursues appropriate measures to correct those laws, policies, and regulations that are not consistent with sound educational goals.
7. Avoids using positions for personal gain through political, social, religious, economic, or other influence.
8. Accepts academic degrees or professional certification only from duly accredited institutions.
9. Maintains the standards and seeks to improve the effectiveness of the profession through research and continuing professional development.
10. Honors all contracts until fulfillment or release.[6]

Acting ethically with integrity and being able to articulate a clear vision are only part of the challenge of becoming a successful principal. An effective administrator must possess certain skills. As suggested earlier, the skills valued in the past are not necessarily those that are expected of today's principal. For much of our educational history, principals were judged on whether they were forceful decision makers. Current building administrators must also make difficult choices, but more and more they are being viewed as facilitators who work well with people. In addition to the management skills necessary in budgeting and scheduling, building leaders must be able to evaluate and coach teachers and have the ability to lead the school in ongoing programs that increase student learning. To do so, they need to have an understanding of child psychology and how children learn.[7] In addition, they are expected to be good listeners and effective public speakers. With a faculty of well-educated teachers, it is also necessary that principals be competent writers. Faculty members will certainly not make light of a principal's grammatical and spelling errors. As the intellectual leader of the building, an administrator will be expected to be able to enter into discussions on current educational research or on pronouncements on education from state or federal level. This is especially true if the school district's vision purports to make the building a true "community of learners."

In seeking to value learning by all, a principal is helping to create a building culture that will provide a challenge to students and faculty alike to continue to increase their own learning. The culture that a principal helps to shape will also affect overall morale in the building. This will undoubtedly affect faculty and staff turnover. One of the biggest current problems in public education is the teacher turnover rate, especially among teachers during their first few years in the profession. Far too many teachers leave teaching after one or two years.

To combat this trend, a principal must attempt to create an environment where teachers feel valued and supported. More than any other area, this support must come from helping teachers with classroom management issues. Faculty members, especially new teachers, hope that building administrators will be able to affect how students behave in their class. For most teachers, sending a student to the office is a last-resort tactic, or it is a result of an emergency in the classroom. They expect that the assistant principal or principal will take the referral seriously. Teachers see administrators not as student counselors, but as the ultimate disciplinarian in a school. Although principals can and should have a positive reputation with students, being sent to the office for disciplinary reasons must be seen by students as something to be avoided.

Along with offering support, the effective principal must make people in the building feel valued. Specific praise for a job well done should be part of the daily work of any administrator. Notes to teachers on special class presentations, an outstanding bulletin board, or merely repeating compliments a principal hears about a teacher or staff member from students or parents will be greatly appreciated. It is equally important that nonteaching personnel receive positive feedback. It is too easy to take the work of secretaries and custodians for granted. Copies of special notes of praise and thanks should also be sent to the direct supervisors of staff members. A custodian who has done an outstanding job preparing for an open house will be happy if the superintendent of buildings and grounds knows about the accomplishment.

In order to be able to be aware of positive accomplishments in the building, a principal must spend a significant portion of each week in the halls and classrooms. The entire school community notices a principal's visibility during the school day, after school, and at evening events. Failure to be an active participant in school life can lead to an administrator's isolation. Despite the demands of paperwork and the need to remain current, a principal must be primarily a "people person." Some days this will be difficult; like anyone else, there will be times when school administrators physically are not feeling well or when they are experiencing significant stress. Like the teacher in the classroom, "the show must go on" and principals must attempt to always portray a positive image. A principal who greets everyone with a smile and a good word will help to set the tone in the building. It is important not to just say hello, but to take the time for conversation. The principal who knows the names of students, faculty, and staff and takes an interest in their lives will more likely earn not only their affection but also their respect. The ability to talk to a student about his or her interest in school will help to create lasting relationships. When one quizzes former students about their school principals, there are several typical responses. Unfortunately, some students will say that they only saw their principal at assemblies, while others will comment that their building administrator seemed to be everywhere and that he or she "even knew my name and what activities I was involved in."

At class reunions, even fifty years after they have graduated, former students will recall positive and negative experiences with their school principals. For most students and faculty, these were important moments in their lives, and principals must always be cognizant that their words and actions in dealing with others are important to these individuals. This fact places a great deal of responsibility on a building administrator, but it also offers a real opportunity to make a difference in the lives of others. Most older and retired building administrators will have conversations with former students, faculty, or staff in which they are directly quoted in conversations that took place many years ago. Even though the principal does not remember the conversation, for the student or staff member, it was important enough to be remembered for years.

While dispensing frequent praise and appreciation is essential, it is equally necessary that principals be skillful at holding others accountable. If someone is frequently tardy or absent without legitimate cause, the principal must confront the problem. There is a skill involved in holding people accountable without destroying their self-esteem. If one has developed respect and trust within the school, it is easier, but it will never be a principal's favorite task. Even more difficult is the need, on infrequent occasions, to end an employee's work within the building. Although this may be the single most dreaded part of the job for most principals, it is a part of the job. Firing someone can be done in a humane fashion. In many cases, the best approach is to urge the individual to resign on the basis that the particular job in this school is just not "the right fit" for this person. It should be the goal, even with an employee who is being dismissed, to minimize resentment and to keep the person from losing totally his or her self-respect and dignity.

One of the ways to avoid turnover of any kind is to give to all employees opportunities for positive staff development. Such programs not only help to improve job performance but they also demonstrate that the school district cares about helping employees to do a better job. These times should also offer opportunities for socialization and team activities. Just as principals should help to arrange professional growth activities for other employees, they should also be involved themselves in obtaining new knowledge and skills. In a survey of secondary principals, the most pressing needs that were identified were "conflict resolution, mediation/negotiation processes" and "empowerment/supportive teachers (e.g., motivating, delegating)."[8] The areas in which principals are seeking additional training will change, but the need for administrators to continue to learn will undoubtedly only increase.

One of the best ways to improve job performance is to receive feedback from others on one's strengths and weaknesses. The practice of gaining feedback for principals has been neglected in many school districts. Even though principals might have some feelings for what is being said about them in the faculty room or in the student lunchroom, teachers and students are most often not a part of any formalized assessment process. Where assessment for principals does occur, it most often primarily occurs during a nontenured administrator's probationary period. Even then, the evaluation might be only that of the superintendent or the assistant superintendent.

With the advent of high-stakes testing, principals are increasingly being judged by the test results of the students in their schools. As suggested earlier, there are many reasons why this as a sole or even major criteria for the evaluation of a principal may be unfair. The fact that schools can and should be doing much more than preparing students for tests suggests that other criteria should be considered. One approach is for principals to maintain a personal portfolio to document their work and accomplishments. Among the entries in such a portfolio might be examples that demonstrate the principal's ability to:

- Show genuine interest in others.
- Respect the thinking of others in formal and informal situations.
- Invite ideas and thoughts for improving the educational arena for learners.
- Work for better human relations among individuals of different racial groups, nationalities, and socioeconomic levels.
- Conduct a survey of teachers, parents, and the lay public in determining the kind of school curriculum desired for students.
- Do an independent study on the role of the school principal; implement those ideas deemed valuable as a professional in the school setting.
- Keep diary and log entries on classroom visitations to observe and assess the quality of teaching in ongoing lessons and units of study; assist teachers to overcome difficulties in teaching based on observations made.
- Conduct action research projects in which the results will be used to improve instruction.
- Write articles for publication in education journals; research for the article needs to pertain to areas of in-service education, thus making the principalship into a true profession.[9]

Such portfolios can be used in evaluation conversations between the principal and his or her direct supervisor.

Whether it is done with portfolios or some sort of rating form, any evaluation instrument should be tied to the mission of the district, as well as to specific long- and short-term objectives. Perhaps the best way that any organization can ensure that goals will be met is to closely relate their accomplishment to the evaluation process. Neil Shipman, director of the

Interstate School Leaders Licensure Consortium (ISLLC) for the Council of Chief State School Officers, has written that, "The systems for evaluating teachers are better in most cases than they are for evaluating principals. . . . The tools and approaches people use are 'just all over the map.'"[10] Another authority on administrative assessment, Pete Reed, reports that, "School districts in most states have the autonomy to determine what principal evaluation will look like and who will carry it out."[11]

Any plan for assessing principals should periodically give the building administrator the opportunity to be reviewed by all of the employees within the building. Any feedback, whether it is from the superintendent or faculty, should be more than a rating scale. Very often the written comments of others will be the most helpful. Principals might wish to develop their own surveys in order to personally identify those areas they wish considered by others. If this is done, a principal should be prepared for both positive and negative feedback. The criticisms might be interpreted by the principal as being unfair or prejudiced; sometimes, they are. On the other hand, if a number of individuals identify a weakness, the wise administrator will accept that a perception is present and that corrective action should be undertaken. It is obvious that no leader will be able to satisfy everyone within an organization and that criticism is inevitable. Even so, it is important to highlight the fact that many people do find success and fulfillment in a career as a building administrator. The opportunity is there to gain the appreciation of one's entire community.

The city of Washington, D.C., has a school district that perhaps offers some of the greatest challenges to building principals. The *Washington Post* decided to honor some of the outstanding administrators in their city. This recognition was based on recommendations from individuals connected with their schools. An article in the newspaper points out some of the characteristics of those who were selected.

- By the accounts and descriptions of those who recommended them, the winners are optimistic, enthusiastic leaders and administrators, generally collaborative and democratic in style, ready to listen to their staffs, students, and parents.
- In addition, leadership traits of the winners appeared to include innovation and creativity.

- Winning principals found ways to stop bullying. "If someone was being picked on and had no friend," a student wrote, Principal Paul R. Rhodes would "help you find a friend and stop being picked on."
- One of the leadership secrets of the winners appeared to be a willingness to pitch in. Maria L. Tukeva, principal of Bell Multicutural Senior High School in the district, was described as someone who, among her other contributions, "waxes the floors when needed."[12]

Those who have been recognized and honored in their district and, in some cases, whose names have been given to school buildings, can see the fact that principals are appreciated and often loved by their communities. Even after retirement, principals are frequently singled out as guests at alumni banquets, class reunions, and retirement parties. It is a job that has many rewards, but it also is one that exacts a high level of commitment. This commitment can affect other aspects of one's life, including the personal life of a principal.

NOTES

1. Rick DuFour, "Challenging Role: Playing the Part of Principal Stretches One's Talent," *Journal of Staff Development*, Fall 1999, at www.nsdc.org/library/jsd/dufour204.html (accessed 17 December 2002).

2. Bess Keller, "Principal Matters," *Education Week*, 11 November 1998, at www.edweek.com/ew/vol-18/11prin.h18 (accessed 17 December 2002).

3. Lee G. Bolman and Terrence E. Deal, "Leading with Soul and Spirit," *The School Administrator Web Edition*, February 2002, at www.aasa.org/publications/sa/2002_02/bolman.htm (accessed 21 February 2003).

4. Bolman and Deal, "Leading with Soul and Spirit."

5. Michael Fullan, "Moral Purpose Writ Large," *The School Administrator Web Edition*, September 2002, at www.aasa.org/publications/sa/2002_09/fullan.htm (accessed 21 February 2003).

6. National Association of Elementary School Principals, "Statement of Ethics for School Administrators," *National Association of Elementary School Principals Policy Statement*, 29 September 1976, at www.naesp.org/ethics.htm (accessed 1 February 2003).

7. Eleanor Chute, "Good Principals Need a Wide Array of Skills," *Post-Gazette.Com*, 22 August 1999, at www.post-gazette.com/regionstate/19990822Train7.asp (accessed 1 February 2003).

8. Regina M. Foley, "Professional Development Needs of Secondary School Principals of Collaborative-Based Service Delivery Models," *Education* 85, no. 1 (October/November 2001): 10–23.

9. Marlow Ediger, "Assessing the School Principal," *Education* 123, no. 1 (Fall 2002): 90–95.

10. John Franklin, "Evaluating the Principal: Changing the Process for Changing Roles," *Education Update*, December 2000, at www.ascd.org/publications/ ed_update/200112/franklin.html (accessed 10 June 2003).

11. Franklin, "Evaluating the Principal."

12. Martin Weil, "Post Honors Principals for Drive, Leadership," *Washington Post.Com*, 19 November 2002, at www.washingtonpost.com/ac2/wp-dyn/ A7879-2002Nov18?language=printer (accessed 13 January 2003).

⓮

THE PRINCIPAL'S PERSONAL LIFE

The first question a new principal must face after taking on the position of a building administrator is to choose where to live. At one time, boards of education expected their administrators to be school district residents. Some rural districts even provided houses for their principals. Although few principals are now required to reside in the school district in which they work, there is little question that many boards of education members and parents would prefer their administrators to be district residents. There are a number of advantages for those principals who choose to live in the district where they work.

To begin with, administrators living closer to their school will save time and money because they will not be commuting long distances. Free time is limited in a principal's life, and an hour saved each day in travel time can provide an administrator more time to engage in other activities. Of course, there are those who will say that they use their driving time constructively in planning or merely unwinding. Others point to the advantage district residents have in keeping track of the pulse of the community. Principals who live in the district will have frequent opportunities to meet and converse with students and parents in the supermarket, coffee shop, or at church functions. People will be more apt to feel that they can approach a principal whom they see often. They also might feel more comfortable making a telephone call to principals at their homes. These administrators believe that living in the district helps them to do a better job because they are more aware of what people are feeling about school issues.

Some principals see such daily contacts as being disruptive to their private lives and feel that it would be like living in a fish bowl if they lived in the same neighborhood as their students and parents. These people fear that they will always be on display and would have to dress appropriately even when making a quick run to the store or worry about drinking a beer at the bowling alley. Some would be concerned that members of the community would be keeping track of their church attendance or their lack of participation in community activities.

Those administrators who are parents have another issue. Some community members might feel that an administrator whose children were attending their school might be more committed than one sending their sons or daughters to another school. Because such administrators appear to have more at stake, parents could believe that they would be more concerned than a "carpetbagger" who comes in from outside the district. Increasingly, principals do worry about the pressure their children and perhaps their spouse would encounter as a result of residing in the district where he or she works. Other family members will also be on display, and it will fall to the spouse to represent the family at parent-teacher conferences and open houses. Some of the children's peers are likely to suggest that children of the principal receive special treatment. The principal's family, on the other hand, might be concerned that the community is holding the children to a higher standard. It is true that if a principal's child is guilty of any significant misbehavior, it will soon be a topic of conversation within the school district. Some sensitive children do not appreciate being the son or daughter of the principal; for others, it is not really a problem.

As a professional employed by the community, there will also be an expectation that school administrators become members of civic organizations and become active in charity campaigns. Principals who live in the community can more easily spend an evening a week at a Rotary or Kiwanis club meeting. Such activities allow administrators to make contacts in the business community, which can be helpful to their schools. The same advantage is available for those principals who choose to worship at a church, mosque, or synagogue in their own school district. Attending the Memorial Day parade and other community activities can give a school administrator additional opportunities to be part of their school district. For many, there is comfort in being able to sink roots into a community, as it does offer a feeling of belonging and helps to create a sense of continuity in one's life.

Increasingly, many principals wish to separate their personal life from their professional work. Along with activities and acquaintances within the district, they have another life in the community in which they live. These administrators find it advantageous to put their job behind them during their free time. They do not want to play the role of school principal for twenty-four hours every day. Instead, they wish to step off the stage when they leave work and have the additional freedom that comes from living outside the school district.

There are economic factors to be considered as well. Unfortunately, there are some wealthy suburban districts where even the school principals cannot afford to live. There are also poor communities that have a very limited number of appropriate housing opportunities for school administrators.

Because many administrators have spouses who also have a full-time job, this issue can also affect where a couple or family chooses to reside. If administrators' spouses do have a job, it is essential that there be a joint decision on who will commute and how far. This decision can easily determine the location of a family's residence. All of the above factors must be kept in mind when a new principal is deciding where to live. It is a topic that should be discussed as part of the interview process to determine the feelings of the board of education and the superintendent. Most important for those principals who do have a spouse is the fact that any decision must be made jointly.

Perhaps the greatest single factor in considering the personal life of a principal is the challenge of time management. Because of the nature of the position and the number of hours necessary to do the job each week, a principal will undoubtedly spend more time carrying out the responsibilities of the position than is typical of most workers. Principals can expect to be out of the home in the evenings for student activities, committee meetings, and possibly sessions of the board of education. Additional after-hours commitments are likely for those principals who become active in community or church organizations. In addition, it will not be unusual for a principal to take home paperwork in the evening. There will be the need to write reports on teacher observations and staff evaluation forms, construct agendas, and prepare for meetings and presentations. Those tasks that are performed in the evening will present a special challenge for the increasing number of women principals who have growing children. Most women principals have neither the time nor the energy to manage a school and to assume the traditional woman's role in the home. A principal who is also a mother can more easily survive the time crunch if she has a husband who accepts a significant share of the household and parenting responsibilities. Whether the principal is a woman or a man, time with one's family must continue to be a top priority. A marriage that is a true partnership will make it possible for principals with a family to do their job without neglecting those closest to them.

As children grow, there will be dance recitals, concerts, athletic events, and other activities of their own children that parents should attend. Doing so demonstrates to the children a parent's love and concern. Choices between attending a school or community meeting and being present at your child's honor society induction will have to be faced. Principals who have missed most of their children's activities have often regretted it.

Family meals together are also important. Despite the hectic schedule of both parents and children, conversations at the dinner table may be one of the few times when families actually talk to each other. Other members of a principal's family should not be neglected. Time must be made to visit parents, brothers and sisters, and other relatives. It is a mistake to let any job come between those who should be closest to us.

Principals will have many acquaintances, both in and out of school. Because the principal is the chief manager in a school building, close friendships with employees can be difficult. Although such friendships can and do exist, many school administrators prefer to develop relationships with those in their community organizations, their neighborhood, or their church or synagogue. Principals in one's own and other districts also can become friends. The challenge again is time. Friendships must be nurtured in order to mature. Busy school administrators must be willing to take the time to do things with friends in order to create a friendship that is real and lasting.

One of the chief cautions a principal must consider in any relationship with family and friends is the need to maintain confidentiality. There are school matters that should not be talked about at a neighborhood picnic or even at the family dinner table. Principals who share information with their spouses must ensure that confidentiality is maintained. Especially for administrators who live in the district, there will be those members of the community who will wish to discuss school matters. Whenever principals speak about a school issue, even in an informal conversation over a cup of coffee, their words are bound to be repeated in the community.

Effectively managing one's time, especially during a principal's first year, will be difficult. During that period, there will be invitations to speak to community groups, as well as to join local service organizations. Any administrator would be prudent to weigh carefully becoming part of a local Kiwanis, Rotary, or other service club during the first year on the job. These organizations meet weekly, either at lunch or dinner. Taking time out each week for a luncheon meeting certainly will cut into an administrator's workweek, while a dinner meeting every Tuesday night becomes just another night out. These groups also engage in service projects, which involve additional committee meetings or weekend projects. There is no doubt that civic organizations make valuable contributions to a community and sometimes to the school district, but a new school administrator should experience at least one year on the job before considering such an obligation. To join and then miss a significant number of meetings because of school conflicts could be worse than initially declining membership. School administrators will be sought after to participate in a number of community activities. When choosing to become involved, it should be something that is not only politically beneficial to the school district but also of interest to the administrator.

To maintain their own physical and mental well-being, school administrators also need to include time in their schedules to exercise. In this regard, many schools offer the advantage of a weight room, a track, or perhaps a swimming pool. Whether it is swimming, jogging, walking, or weight lifting, principals need to give exercise a high priority in their daily lives. Ideally, an exercise program should include a variety of physical activities, but in any case, it must be regular. An early morning walk or jog with a family member or friend is a good way to begin the day. If morning is not an ideal time, it will be necessary to schedule an alternative time at the end of the day. Too many school administrators fail to take care of their own physical needs, which include not only exercise but also good nutrition and getting enough sleep.

Finally, it is easy for principals to become one-dimensional people. They become so focused on their jobs that they think or talk of little else. It is a positive thing for one's mental health to have interests outside of work. Whether it is collecting stamps, restoring cars, or camping, people in demanding jobs need other outlets. Intellectually, we need to read outside of the field of education. Fiction, biography, and history books can only broaden us and make us more interesting people. Administrators need these additional interests to keep from becoming boring people and also to enrich their own lives.

In order to maintain their ability to be positive leaders, principals should take the vacation time that is allotted to them. There are administrators who worry that the school cannot function if they take more than a few days off at a time. This is often not true; if a school is so dependent on one person, changes should take place within the organization that remedy such a situation. For many administrators, the best way to truly have a vacation is to leave the district in order to escape the telephone and other potential interruptions.

Vacations are just one way to deal with the stress that occurs when one becomes a principal. School administrators, like others who hold responsible positions, will encounter symptoms of stress at times during their career. Peggy Hinckley writes in the *School Administrator* that, "Before we can successfully manage stress, we need to understand it. Stress is a state of dynamic tension created when we respond to perceived demands and pressures—both internal and external."[1] In that same article, she identifies several of the causes of stress. She first discusses what is called *relationship stress*, about which she writes:

> Are you so busy building relationships with community groups, staff members, and parents that you burn bridges with the significant others in your personal life? Do you attend the conference football championship but miss your daughter's piano recital? Are you so focused on school issues that you don't listen to anything your spouse says?

Relationships are like a garden: Weeds will grow anywhere, but flowers take more effort. Examine your relationships outside the office. Do you tend to them, nurture them and help them grow? Note the health of your relationships with regard to affection, family bonds, social life, and confidantes.[2]

She identifies a second cause of stress as *personal stress*, which she explains this way.

Are you at peace with yourself? Or is your stomach tied in knots? Do you find yourself acting in ways that would make your enemies proud? Inner resiliency is vital to your survival. . . .

Whatever your faith or spiritual beliefs, regular meditation and/or worship can decrease feelings of isolation and abandonment. When a problem seems too great to solve, it is a relief to give that problem to a higher power and listen for an answer.[3]

The article also highlights financial problems in the life of an administrator. In this regard, the author asks "Do you know all the intricate details of your school budget but have no idea where your personal money goes? Money can be a great source of stress, particularly if you feel like you are working harder and not getting ahead financially. Take a look at your spending as well as your organizational habits."[4]

The final source of stress is related to health and Hinckley urges administrators to ask themselves:

Do you leave a board meeting sweating and short of breath? Do you stay awake at night worrying about unresolved issues? Have you increased your alcohol, caffeine, and/or nicotine intake as a response to increased stress? . . .

To balance the toll stress takes on your body, pay close attention to what you eat, how much sleep you get, and what shape your body is in physically.[5]

In dealing with stress and all of the other issues related to a school administrator's personal life, the goal should be to achieve an appropriate balance. Although the job is an important part of who administrators are, they are more than a principal—they are people with families, friends, and outside interests. Anyone will be a more successful educational leader if he or she is a well-rounded, complete human being. Having considered all of the factors mentioned in this and previous chapters, it is appropriate now to attempt to summarize the advantages and disadvantages of a career as a school principal.

NOTES

1. Peggy Hinckley, "When Pigs Fly and Cats Bark," *American Association of School Administrators*, September 2001, at www.aasa.org/publications/sa/2001_09/hinckley.htm (accessed 21 February 2003).
2. Hinckley, "When Pigs Fly."
3. Hinckley, "When Pigs Fly."
4. Hinckley, "When Pigs Fly."
5. Hinckley, "When Pigs Fly."

⓳

THE ADVANTAGES AND
DISADVANTAGES OF THE POSITION

Many potential candidates for administrative leadership positions are discouraged by their understanding of the schedules that school principals must keep. It is not only the late afternoon and evening meetings that bother possible future administrators, but the days worked during school vacations. While teachers are usually contracted to work ten months, a principal's schedule usually involves a twelve-month commitment, with three or four weeks of paid vacation. Administrators are also expected to be at work during winter and spring vacations, unless they choose to use some of their vacation time during these breaks. Teachers, especially those with families, treasure the extensive vacations, even if they have to take work home during these breaks. Taking on more work days is seen as a serious disadvantage for many teachers who might consider administration.

On the other hand, administrators often enjoy and appreciate their jobs during the times when students and teachers are on vacation. It is an opportunity for catching up, and it can be a more relaxing and an informal change of pace for principals. Many principals remember that as teachers they had needed to take on lower paying and less satisfying jobs during the summer to supplement their incomes. Many see having a twelve-month salary as an advantage.

Salaries are another concern of those teachers who are not willing to consider administration. Although principals and assistant principals usually receive higher yearly salaries than the highest paid teachers, if one were to calculate the difference by determining a daily or hourly wage, it could be concluded that ten-month teachers are being compensated more richly than the twelve-month administrator. This is especially true for assistant principals, who might even take a reduction in salary when leaving the classroom for their first administrative job. Still, it is true that salaries for administrators are increasing at a slightly higher percentage rate than those for teachers. "Principals are paid, on average, 66 percent more than teachers on the basis of average annual salary, but a principal's work year is typically 20 percent longer than a teacher's. As a result, principals actually make approximately 33 percent more per day ($323.94 as compared to $233.35) than teachers."[1]

Those teachers concerned about salary also point to the fact that managers with comparable responsibilities in the private sector are paid much higher salaries than school principals. With salaries and stock options, one study concluded that middle managers in the private sector are making approximately $40,000 per year more than the average school principal.[2] Even with this fact, it is also true that most public employees enjoy an excellent retirement plan, as well as significant assistance in paying for their health insurance. There is also evidence, especially as there are expected to be fewer qualified candidates, that school administrative salaries will continue to rise.

Perhaps more than salaries, those teachers who are skeptical about becoming a principal point to the politics involved in the field of administration. For many people, politics is a word with a negative connotation; however, if one thinks of politics as the process for making decisions, it can be seen as a necessary and important part of the functioning of any organization. In a democracy, decisions need to be made with the "advice and consent" of a large number of constituents. It is true that a middle manager, such as a principal, must work with the board of education and central administration and also maintain the trust and respect of teachers, staff, students, and parents. It is inevitable that these groups will sometimes disagree. This is especially true with employee unions and the board of education. A principal must accept the situation as a reality, but it certainly does not make the job impossible. Finding ways to meld the interests and aspirations of all of these groups is a challenge that a building leader can enjoy. Working with a school advisory committee consisting of teachers, students, parents, and even board members to accomplish worthwhile projects can be a rewarding experience for any educational leader.

Especially since the added accountability arising from high-stakes testing, some have pointed out that principals are being held responsible for test results, even though they lack the power within the organization to bring about needed changes in their schools. Although there is reason for concern, especially in some districts, there currently seems to be a trend toward giving individual schools more responsibility in the areas of budget, curriculum materials, and personnel choices. Even with the concept of site-based management, which requires principals to use shared decision-making processes, there is a growing consensus that principals need to be empowered.

Another aspect of the job that frightens some potential candidates is that principals must frequently deal with conflict situations. Whether it is a problem between students, a teacher and a student, a parent and a teacher, or even two employees, it frequently is the role of the principal to mediate or sometimes be the arbitrator or the judge in such conflicts. Many of the situations are not simple, and the responsibility for the disagreement does not reside totally with one or another of the protagonists. The principal must approach these sometimes emotional confrontations calmly and attempt to find solutions that are fair and just. At times, the principal is not the person in the middle, but is one of the participants in a dispute. Unions will file grievances on certain actions taken by the building administrator, and parents will sometimes react harshly to a principal's decision. It is difficult not to take such grievances and complaints as personal criticism, but it is all part of the job. A teacher considering administration should know that effective administration preparation programs will help prepare students for such situations. Administrators who have been classroom teachers have already had experiences in dealing with conflict. It is a skill that can be developed, and those principals who become effective mediators can reduce disruptive conflicts in their buildings.

In part, the fact that principals are continually dealing with problems makes the job physically and emotionally draining. When an administrator leaves the office at the end of the day, there will usually be unresolved situations that must be faced the next morning. To suggest that it is easy to put these matters aside at the end of a day would be simplifying reality. It is often not possible to avoid lying in bed thinking about difficult problems. Successful administrators develop ways to forget the job long enough to be responsive and positive companions for their family and friends. With time on the job, this can become easier because principals should learn from their experience. After one survives the first negative board of education meeting, public hearing, angry parent, or the task of firing an employee, principals can more easily accept such experiences. It would be naïve for anyone entering school administration to not expect some unpleasantness. At the same time, one must accept the fact that stressful situations can occur in any job and that through appropriate training and experience, principals can become better prepared to deal with problems. Certainly, physically strong and well-adjusted leaders in any field can and will stand up to stressful situations.

An additional worry for teachers moving into administration is the transition from being a faculty member to being a supervisor of others. In the case of the approximately 50 percent of principals appointed within their own building, there is the concern about whether they will be accepted by their former colleagues. Many worry as well about how their elevation to the position of principal will affect their long-term friendships with people in the building. This too is a problem which can and is dealt with successfully by most principals who move into a leadership position in their building. It is likely that the appointment would not have been made if the teacher chosen was not well liked and respected in the school. Superintendents and boards of education tend to be very cautious about choosing someone as a building principal who is not supported by the faculty. The fact is that most teachers and staff members will wish their new principal well and hope for their success. The superintendent and the board who made the selection will certainly want their appointee to do well. For this reason, most principals begin their job with a good deal of support; if a new administrator is willing to listen and to work with others, the transition from teacher to principal can be a smooth one.

An additional concern of those who hesitate to make the move to school administration is the fear that they will no longer be working directly with students. The fact that effective teachers find it a joy to be with their students causes them to be unwilling to give up this vital advantage for a job in administration. Faculty members often think that the principal deals only with those students who have discipline problems. Unfortunately, for some assistant principals, this is too frequently the case. The fact is, principals, if they choose, have ample opportunities to work with and get to know students. A good principal can very easily become acquainted with more students than the typical faculty member who works with a limited number of students.

The truly caring principal is greeting students when they enter school, talking with them in the cafeteria, and modeling effective teaching in the classroom. These contacts do not have to be limited to merely saying "Good morning!" and "How are you doing?" Principals have the flexibility in their schedule to be with students at almost any time they choose. Most middle schools or high schools would be delighted to have their building administrator teach a class each year. If one teaches the first hour of the day, he or she still would have time to complete administrative duties. Student advisory committees and frequent meetings with student government leaders are another way that administrators can get closer to students. Even with disciplinary issues, a student and the principal can develop a mutual respect and a lasting relationship.

At the elementary level, the principal who joins in a classroom game or reads a story to the class becomes a real person in the eyes of the children. Student musicians, actors, and athletes at all levels truly appreciate a principal's interest and support of their activities. There is ample evidence that principals can and do have a positive impact on individual students. Finally, they can be role models for children. This may be especially important for principals who are members of a minority group. It is undoubtedly true that as we have more female principals, young women may more frequently see themselves in the role of a school administrator.

For anyone in education, the most important rewards do come from the experiences with children. The principal can take pride in the accomplishments of all of the children in the building. Students who win regional spelling bees, receive a national merit scholarship, or are accepted by a major university are a source of pride for a building administrator. Perhaps more than most school employees, the principal can become excited about a championship athletic team or a journalism award received by the school newspaper or yearbook. Great satisfaction also comes to the administrator who has helped to introduce a new academic program or if the school's standardized test scores improve from one year to the next.

Although it does not happen everyday, there will be faculty, staff, students, and parents who will extend their thanks for something that a principal has done. There will also be a very positive feeling when a child proudly introduces you to their parents as "my principal." Most school administrators also take pride in the achievements of their former students who go on to make a positive contribution to society. In addition, there are the visits to school by former students who stop by to share their memories and report on their current activities. It is also not unusual for students to honor their principal with a yearbook dedication.

All of the joys of the principalship do not occur when one is working in the position. Retired principals talk of their contacts with former students. Some students may keep in touch for a lifetime through notes and holiday messages. It is not unusual for retired principals to be asked to speak at class reunions or to come back to school to participate in graduation or honor society inductions. Many principals have worked as mentors for those teachers in their building who are seeking to prepare for administration. These relationships can also be lasting and result in lifelong friendships. Being a mentor to future administrators may be one of the most important contributions a principal can make. It is often the principal who first urges a teacher to consider administration. This encouragement can make a difference in a person's life. In making these recommendations, building administrators are helping to select and train the future leaders of our schools.

Not only does a principal affect the career of those considering administration but even more often, they influence the professional development of teachers in their school. Besides demonstrating good teaching, a building principal can often offer encouragement and support when teachers begin to doubt themselves. A principal's actions can determine whether a teacher with great potential stays in or leaves the profession.

Finally, a principal is instrumental in affecting the human relations environment in the school. When the building leader is the right person for the job, schools can be wonderful places for students, faculty, and staff. A school building is very much like an extended family, and it is the principal who helps to set the tone for how people interact. Being the leader of a happy, productive school is an experience that can bring a deep sense of satisfaction. Such a school can be a wonderful place to spend one's time. No school is without problems, but neither is any other workplace. Still, the potential sense of fulfillment and joy available to those who lead a school make it a career that should at least be considered by anyone who thinks he or she might be up to the challenge. Not all teachers should seek a career in administration. For too long, master teachers have left the classroom for the wrong reasons and have regretted their decision. How can one know if the principalship is right for him or her? Help in answering this question is the goal of the final chapter.

NOTES

1. National Association of Elementary School Principals, "School Principals' Salaries Increase, Keep in Step with Teachers," *National Association of Elementary School Principals News*, 6 April 2001, at www.innovations-educ.com/comm/prss4-6-01.htm (accessed 21 February 2003).
2. William G. Cunningham and J. Brent Sperry, "Where's the Beef in Administrator Pay?" *The School Administrator Web Edition*, February 2001, at www.aasa.org/publications/sa/2001_02/cunningham.htm (accessed 21 February 2003).

16

IS THE PRINCIPALSHIP
THE RIGHT JOB FOR ME?

Some teachers have aspired to become a principal since they were students, while others begin to think about it after they become teachers. For these latter individuals, it is often a recommendation of a principal or another faculty member that causes them to think about administration. Whatever motivation causes someone to consider a career as a building principal, he or she should realize that it will require a major commitment. In order to understand what might be required, there are some questions they might ask themselves to assist in making the decision.

1. Am I willing to make the sacrifices in money and time to become certified as a principal? To do so will mean a commitment not only to pay for the college costs, even if it requires borrowing money, but also to the many hours required during the evening, and possibly Saturday, to attend classes. In most states, there will also be requirements for internships that could result in some loss of income.

2. If I am married, do I have the support of my family, not only for the period of preparation but for the changes in family routine that will be necessary when I become a principal? Is my spouse ready and willing to accept additional household and family responsibilities, as well as the idea that I will have additional commitments in the evening?

3. Am I and is my family willing to consider moving to another community in order for me to find my first administrative position?

4. Will I be able to discipline my private life in a way that ensures that I will be an excellent role model for my students, as well as for all of the residents of the school district? Do I realize that the community will carefully monitor my behavior and that of my family?

5. Can I become a lifelong learner who will need to remain current in many more areas than I would as a classroom teacher? Am I really interested in subjects such as curriculum development, assessment, and school law? Will I be able to remain informed on new trends in education, law, and court decisions related to schools?

6. Can I see myself as a mediator in conflict situations? Do I have the backbone to discipline difficult students and employees, to deny tenure to a teacher, or fire a teacher or staff member?

7. Can I avoid moodiness and impulsiveness even when I am feeling stress or suffering from physical discomfort? Will I be able to smile and be of good humor even when under stress?

8. Even though I may not enjoy computers and other technology, will I be able to lead my school in developing and maintaining an effective technology program?

9. Do I have or can I develop the skills necessary to be an effective public speaker, writer, and debater? Will I be able to exercise these skills, even in emotionally charged situations?

10. Will I be able to sleep at night, even though there are complicated and unresolved issues to be dealt with the next day?

11. Am I able to work with multiple issues and problems simultaneously without becoming distracted or frustrated?

12. Is it possible for me to accept compromise and to live with ambiguity?

13. Can I make a decision without causing myself ongoing anguish and constantly second-guessing myself?

14. Do I have the humility to admit mistakes and to "take the heat" when things are going wrong? Will I be willing to take responsibility for failures in my building, even though much of the blame might lie with others? Can I accept the reality that I am accountable for whatever might happen in my school?

15. Am I a good listener who is willing to accept the ideas of others, even if it means I must change my position on an issue?

16. Will I be able to tolerate the inevitable criticism of others, whether it is chatter in the faculty room, letters to the newspaper, or gossip in the community? At the same time, will I learn to use constructive criticism of others from whatever evaluation process of principals is used by my district?

17. Realizing that I will be spending many hours in meetings, will I have the skills and patience to lead and be a constructive participant in the many hours that I will spend in group decision-making sessions?

18. Have I developed at least the beginning of a vision or a dream for what a school should be?

19. Finally, what is my motivation for seeking a job as a principal? Undoubtedly, numerous factors will affect my decision. One major reason for becoming a principal should be a sincere desire to help children. Money, respect, and the prestige of the position are not sufficient reasons to enter the field of administration. Merely seeking to get out of the classroom is also a poor motive. Certainly, a person's motivation will include a mixture of personal aspirations and professional goals, but not all of the motivation should be self-serving. Principals need to have their share of idealism.

Obviously everyone will have areas where, because of their temperament or because of lack of knowledge or experience, they will be weak. These are not easy questions for anyone to answer, especially if one has yet to have any administrative experience. In a way, it is similar to a soldier wondering how he or she will react in combat. Still, most people know themselves well enough to respond to many of these questions. It also might be helpful to share them with people who know you well and who you trust will attempt to truthfully respond in assessing your strengths and weaknesses. If one remains unsure, it can also be helpful to take an introductory administrative course or to have conversations with practicing administrators. Although this process might be helpful and sometimes flattering, potential administrators should not let anyone else talk them into making a career change. Those who take on the position of a building administrator should feel some sort of calling that draws them to the position. Even with such motivation, individuals must enter school administration with their eyes wide open. A principal cannot afford to be naïve about the inevitable pressures of the position. You will be surprised that your powers are less absolute than you anticipate and that you will need to rely on other people to truly make a difference.

Still, for those who do make the decision, the potential for doing good is truly great. You will be joining the ranks of many outstanding men and women, past and present, who have made a difference in their community and in the lives of children. It will not be easy; one is reminded of the comment that John Gardner made on assuming the position of Secretary of Health, Education, and Welfare: "We are continually faced with a series of great opportunities brilliantly disguised as insoluble problems."[1] The problems of the principalship, however daunting, are not insurmountable, and it is essential that in each generation people step forward to accept the challenge of leadership in our schools. So much depends on how well we educate our children. Over 2,000 years ago, Aristotle wrote that "All who have meditated on the art of governing mankind have been convinced that the fate of empires depends on the education of youth."[2]

However important the job is, not all teachers should seek to become principals. Some in the past may well have been victims of the Peter Principle, which was articulated in a best-selling book in 1969. The authors, Laurence J. Peters and Raymond Hull, articulated the following theory: "In a hierarchy, every employee tends to rise to his level of incompetence."[3] One of the book's illustrations of the principle is the story of B. Lunt. This is the story.

> B. Lunt had been a competent student, teacher, and department head, and was promoted to assistant principal. In this post he got on well with teachers, students, and parents, and was intellectually competent. He gained a further promotion to the rank of principal.
>
> Till now, he had never dealt directly with school-board members, or with the district superintendent of education. It soon appeared that he lacked the required finesse to work with these high officials. *He kept the superintendent waiting* while he settled a dispute between two children. Taking a class for a teacher who was ill, *he missed a curriculum revision committee meeting* called by the assistant superintendent.

He worked so hard at running his school that *he had no energy for running community organizations.* He declined offers to become program chairman of the Parent-Teacher Association, president of the Community Betterment League, and consultant to the Committee for Decency in Literature.

His school lost community support and he fell out of favor with the superintendent. Lunt came to be regarded, by the public and his superiors, as an incompetent principal. When the assistant superintendent's post became vacant, the school board declined to give it to Lunt. He remains, and will remain till he retires, unhappy and incompetent as a principal.[4]

As suggested earlier, it is not necessary or even advisable for every good teacher to aspire to be a principal. More important is the message of an often quoted, anonymous statement that says, "One hundred years from now it will not matter what kind of car I drove, what kind of house I lived in, how much was in my bank account, nor what my clothes looked like. But one hundred years from now the world may be a little better because I was important in the life of a child."[5] One can achieve this most noble goal as a classroom teacher or as a principal. Whatever choice is made, one should know that the position of a school principal is an exciting, meaningful, and essential career. The choice is yours.

NOTES

1. "John W. Gardner Famous Quotes," *Thinkexist.com*, at www.thinkexist.com/English/Author/x/Author_4817_1.htm (accessed 10 July 2003).

2. Aristotle in Laurence J. Peter, *Peter's Quotations: Ideas for Our Time* (New York: Bantam, 1977), 161.

3. Laurence J. Peter and Raymond Hull, *The Peter Principle: Why Things Always Go Wrong* (New York: Bantam, 1969), cover.

4. Peter and Hull, *The Peter Principle*, 13–14.

5. Anonymous, "A Little Inspiration," *A Little Inspiration*, at http://webhome.idirect.com/~qdsouza/inspiration2.htm (accessed 10 July 2003).

INDEX

academic achievement, 6

ADHD. *See* attention deficit hyperactivity

administrative training programs: aspiring principals' programs, 30, 37; certification programs and requirements, 20–22, 30–32; internships, 15, 17; LEARN, 17; *Learning to Lead, Learning to Learn: Improving School Quality through Principal Professional Development*, 17–18; problem-based learning, 16; training programs, 15, 17–20; urban areas, 23–24

alternate educational services. *See* National Association of Elementary School Principals

aspiring principals' program. *See* administrative training programs

assertive discipline, 94

assistant principal. *See* principal

attention deficit hyperactivity, 73–74

board of education, 51; budget, 52–53; hiring, 38–41, 157, 159; legal challenges, 143; negotiations, 3, 53–54; pressures, conflicting, 3; references, as, 32; relationships with, 5; school law, 133, 143; security, 91; viewing teachers as candidates, 29; working with, 52–55, 166, 168. *See also* trends in public education, major

booster clubs, 74

Brown vs. Topeka, Kansas, 132

Buckley Amendment. *See* Family Educational Rights and Privileges Act (FERA)

budget. *See* board of education

building manager. *See* principal

candidates: appointment of, 38–40; female, 37–38; minority, 37–38; preparation of, 40–43

Canter, Lee, 94

censorship, 142

ABOUT THE AUTHOR

Bill Hayes has been a high school social studies teacher, department chair, assistant principal, and high school principal. From 1973–1994, he served as superintendent of schools for the Byron-Bergen Central School District, which is located eighteen miles west of Rochester, New York. During his career, he was an active member of the New York State Council of School Superintendents and is the author of a council publication entitled *The Superintendency: Thoughts for New Superintendents*, which is used to prepare new superintendents in New York State.

Mr. Hayes has also written a number of articles for various education journals. Since his retirement in 1994, he has chaired the Teacher Education Division at Roberts Wesleyan College in Rochester, New York. He is the author of *Real-Life Case Studies for Teachers*, *Real-Life Case Studies for School Administrators*, *So You Want to Be a Superintendent?*, *So You Want to Be a School Board Member?*, *Real-Life Case Studies for School Board Members*, and *So You Want to Be a College Professor?*.